Choices: You Make 'em You Own 'em

Choices You Make 'em You Own 'em

Rage, Regrets, Redemption

The Jerry Tillinghast Story

Written by Joe Broadmeadow as told by Jerry Tillinghast

Also by Joe Broadmeadow

A Change of Hate

Silenced Justice

Collision Course

Saving the Last Dragon

Run

Scream

Published by Jebwizard Publishing

USA

ISBN-13:978-1718148611

The Right to Remain Silent

Time:

Date:

I, **Jerry Tillinghast**, having been informed that I am best known as a **Reputed Mob Enforcer**, voluntarily, without threats or promises on the part of anyone, make this statement to the world.

I have the right to remain silent. If I give up the right to remain silent, I can stop at any time.

After having been informed of my constitutional rights, I do understand these rights, and I agree to give a statement.

Everything you are about to read is the truth.

I have the right to remain silent and the right to be

SILENT NO MORE...

Thank you for reading this book. I hope you enjoy the story and learn something about the choices you make and accepting the consequences.

Choices: You Make 'em You Own 'em

_____

Jerry Tillinghast

_____

Joe Broadmeadow

Dedication

The genesis of this book was the brainchild of Jerry Tillinghast's friend, Larry Cunningham. Larry, after convincing Jerry of the concept, reached out to the late Glenn Laxton, reporter extraordinaire from WPRI Channel 12.

Glenn understood men like Jerry were one-dimensional in the public's perception, Illuminated by the harsh light of news headlines while shadows hid the rest of the story.

A story that needed telling.

Glenn covered many stories about organized crime; the killings, the trials, the rise and fall of the Patriarca era. No one had ever tried to tell the story about how men like Jerry Tillinghast chose such a way of life.

No one had ever thought to ask Jerry to tell his whole story. Glenn's credibility and reputation were the catalysts that convinced Jerry to begin the process.

For Glenn's insightfulness in recognizing that a person is more than the public perception, more than an overused sobriquet, more than notorious and feared, we dedicate this book.

Without Glenn's vision, most people would never know the whole story of Jerry Tillinghast. For that, we are eternally grateful.

We would also dedicate this book to Linda Laxton, Glenn's wife, who provided all of Glenn's notes and research making the completed book possible.

Without Glenn and Linda, this story could not be told. While Glenn passed away before he could finish the project, his efforts are reflected within the chapters.

Jerry Tillinghast
Joe Broadmeadow

Foreword

I first met Gerald M. 'Jerry' Tillinghast in Attorney Paul Dimaio's office on July 31, 2017. Yet it was not the first time I'd heard of him. As the son of a Rhode Island State Trooper, many names of the mob guys they pursued were familiar. Then they were just names and reputations although some of mythical proportions. A mix of media hype and the ominous shadow cast by organized crime.

Jerry is a bear of a man. Even as he's gathered over seventy-two birthdays, there is strength in his handshake. One can feel the muscle in his fingers.

He is also disarmingly charming, funny, and quick-witted.

The Jerry Tillinghast I met is someone you could enjoy having a beer with sitting in a pub. But from 1978 to 2011, he wasn't available. He was in a cell in the Adult Correctional Institution, known as the ACI, serving life for murder. For my entire career as a police officer in the East Providence Police Department, Jerry was in prison.

Paul Dimaio, one of the most respected criminal defense lawyers in Rhode Island, has a long association with Jerry and his late brother Harold Tillinghast. Their relationship stretched from casual drinks at a bar, to representing Jerry in one of the most significant criminal cases in Rhode Island, Bonded Vault. Paul also was a potential key witness in the murder trial that put Jerry and Harold away for life.

A witness no one ever put on the stand.

This is the whole story of Gerald 'Jerry' Tillinghast. Not just the 'feared mob enforcer' for the Patriarca Crime family.' Not the suspect in several unsolved homicides. Not just the convicted murderer.

Not just the man who, by the mere mention of his name, could strike terror into the heart of men accustomed to violence.

This is the story of how Jerry Tillinghast went from the streets of South Providence to the killing fields of Vietnam to a cell at the Adult Correctional Institution. This is the whole story about Jerry Tillinghast of Providence, Rhode Island. The man behind the reputation.

What compels a man to a life where everything else, friends, family, and yourself, come second? Jerry found a father figure in Raymond Patriarca, as strong as any biological one, who bound him to absolute loyalty.

Loyalty he maintains to this day.

This is not your typical wiseguy turned storyteller trying to bolster his image and minimize his past. This is not, to paraphrase Nicholas Pileggi in *Wiseguy* the definitive book on organized crime, "the egomaniacal ravings of an illiterate hood masquerading as a benevolent godfather."

Before the conviction that put him away on a life sentence, authorities charged him in several murders and conspiracy cases.

All dismissed.

He was arrested and charged in the infamous Bonded Vault Robbery case.

He would be found not guilty at trial.

This is how he reached the highs and lows in a life of crime, did his time, fathered several children while behind bars, and attended college as he approached his 70th birthday; earning thirty-six credits toward his degree.

This is the story of how a chance encounter in a New Hampshire prison led him to discover and embrace Wicca and the pagan doctrine.

This is a story of opportunity wasted, denied, or ignored.

This is a story of redemption. This is the Jerry Tillinghast few have ever met.

Still in Saigon

Songwriters: Dan Dailey
Still in Saigon lyrics © Asilomar Music

'Got on a plane in Fresco and got off in Vietnam.
I walked into a different world, the past forever gone.
I could have gone to Canada or I could have stayed in school.
But I was brought up differently. I couldn't break the rules.
Thirteen months and fifteen days, the last ones were the worst.
One minute I kneel down and pray and the next I stand and curse.
No place to run to where I did not feel that war.
When I got home I stayed alone and checked behind each door.
Still in Saigon
Still in Saigon
I am Still in Saigon in my mind!
The ground at home was covered with snow. And I was covered in sweat.
My younger brother calls me a killer and My daddy calls me a vet.
Everybody says that I'm someone else That I'm sick and there's no cure.
Damned if I know who I am. There was only one place I was sure
When I was

Still in Saigon

Still in Saigon.

I am still in Saigon in my mind!

Every summer when it rains, I smell the jungle, I hear the planes.

I can't tell no one I feel ashamed. Afraid someday I'll go insane.

That's been ten long years ago and time has gone on by.

But now and then I catch myself

Eyes searchin' through the sky.

All the sounds of long ago will be forever in my head.

Mingled with the wounded's cries and the silence of the dead

'Cause I'm

Still in Saigon

Still in Saigon

I am still in Saigon in my mind

Chapter 1   *November 30, 1978*

One Tale, Two Stories

The stolen car made its way along the side streets of Cranston, Rhode Island onto Interstate 95 South. Cloudy and drizzly, the winds of November cast a pall over the night. Three men, two in the front seat one in the back, came together for a single purpose that evening.

Or so they believed.

One knew it was a deadly deception.

As the car sped up, other vehicles followed behind. Three undercover police units, two driven by detectives from the Rhode Island State Police and one by an FBI agent.

The stolen car took the Airport Connector exit in Warwick toward T. F. Green Airport. The police surveillance team followed behind. As the vehicle negotiated the corner, the cops lost sight of it. Their view blocked, for just a few seconds, by a snow fence along the roadway.

Different today than it was in 1978, the curving off-ramp put cars right onto Post Road. The police regained sight of the of the vehicle as it waited at the red light.

Just two men, both in the front seat, are now visible in the car. Uncertain if they had dropped off the third man, or spotted the surveillance team, the police watched the vehicle turn onto Post Road and then down a side street into an industrial area. They backed off and waited.

After several minutes, the cops moved into the area.

It didn't take long to find what they were looking for.

FBI Agent Phil Reilly spotted the car first and called for State Police Lieutenant Vincent Vespia. The two approached the car, noticing the windows steaming up. As they peered in the window, they saw George Basmajian, the primary object of their surveillance, lying on the back seat, dead or dying from bullet wounds to the head and chest. The medical examiner would later count nine bullet wounds, several of which were likely fatal.

Nine shots were a guarantee of fatality.

No one else was around. The other men had vanished into the night. The cops knew who they needed to look for and headed out to find them.

And this is where the story diverges. But to understand the differences and perspective, we must return to the beginning. To go back to the routes of involvement of those connected to this case through their early choices and associations with organized crime.

Routes of Involvement

It was the best of times for the Providence-based Patriarca organized crime family. It was the worst of times for the cops and federal agents tasked with investigating them.

Raymond Loreda Salvatore Patriarca, Sr., led the organization with ruthless and absolute power. During the turbulent 60s and 70s in Rhode Island, Patriarca controlled a far-reaching criminal empire. It protected itself through the deliberate corruption of politicians, cops, and judges. Patriarca's reputation within organized crime extended far beyond Rhode Island. He controlled the Boston-based Angiulo crime organization. His reach stretched to New York where his influence held sway over the five major New York families.

Organized crime in Providence, based on the Italian Mafia model, was in its heyday and Patriarca was the king. How does a sixty-plus-year-old man strike fear by the mere mention of his name? By surrounding himself with men who would die before betraying him. Men willing and able to kill anyone on Patriarca's word without the slightest hesitation. Men who would forsake everything to protect the organization.

While becoming a "made" member of this organization required Italian heritage, becoming useful to Raymond did not.

His power came from a devote group of handpicked men. If Patriarca had his faults, he also had his strengths. He inspired loyalty from those around him. Few made the mistake of betraying his trust.

Betrayal was always costly, and often fatal.

In 1975, having returned to Rhode Island pending his release from federal prison for one of his few criminal convictions, Patriarca sets in motion one of the most successful robberies in Rhode Island history. A crime motivated not just by greed, that was a bonus, but by that same iron rule of respect ignored by those who remained free while Raymond sat in prison. Those associates who, benefiting from the organization built by Patriarca, forgot to pay proper respect to the founder of their feast.

It would cost them.

Jerry's loyalty to the code of silence would cost him. He will tell you it cost his brother Harold a great deal more. But recognizing the fallacy of a long-held belief, one seared into your

3

being almost from the moment of birth, takes time and perspective.

In Jerry's case, it took almost thirty years in prison and lonely times of soul-searching and deep contemplation in a cell before he came to understand. This is the story of Jerry from the streets of Providence to the jungles of Vietnam to his life in the mob. His journey of rage, regrets, and redemption.

"Three Things Cannot Long Be Hidden; the Sun, the Moon, and the Truth."

Buddhist saying

Until now, most people learned the story of the murder of George Basmajian on November 30, 1978, from newspaper reports about the arrest and trial of brothers Jerry and Harold Tillinghast.

By the end of that evening, one man would be dead and two others on their way to a life sentence for murder.

The story of that fateful night played out in the media for the next few days and culminated in the trial of Jerry and Harold in July 1979. The specter of a mob-sanctioned hit by Raymond L.S. Patriarca, the feared boss of the New England organized crime, handled by the crew of his unofficial second-in-command, Gerard 'The Frenchman' Ouimette, hovered over the proceedings.

All these elements combine into a tantalizing story. Two reputed enforcers for organized crime, Jerry Tillinghast and George Basmajian, members of Gerard Ouimette's volatile crew, along with Jerry's brother Harold, being followed by the elite investigators of the Rhode Island State Police and the FBI and ending with one man shot nine times; dead in the back of a stolen car.

Unanswered questions linger from that time.

Why did the State Police and FBI pick that day to follow Basmajian? Was there an informant who tipped them that something was in the works? Or was it something else? Was there another source placed in an opportune location to hear things not meant for the ears of law enforcement?

Or was it a fortuitous choice made by seasoned and intelligent investigators that men such as Basmajian were never far from the next score? That following him was a useful investigative tool.

Choices made by different men that sent them on a collision course ending in murder for one, life in prison for two, and the case of a lifetime for the cops.

Throughout the entire travel of this case, from the moment of his arrest to the moment he walked out of prison almost three decades later, Jerry Tillinghast has said just one thing about that night; Harold was not in the car.

He has offered nothing more than that; still clinging to the long-dispelled myth of the code of silence. Like all stories told from memory, old police reports, and conflicting trial testimony, the truth is often clouded and murky.

For the first time since that damp, cold November night, Jerry reveals the whole story. Time has taken its toll on his conscience. The fall of once legendary mobsters, brought on by the testimony of other mobsters, has exposed the lie that is the code of silence.

Since that November night, Jerry has come to terms with his choices. He fought through the rage, learned to live with the regrets, and found a path to redemption.

Is this a tale of misplaced loyalty based on a debunked code of silence, or something more? Understanding men like Jerry, and the choices they make, is best accomplished by starting at the beginning.

This is the story of how Jerry Tillinghast earned a reputation for brutality, power, and respect within the insular world of the Mafia. A secretive world that granted Jerry partial admission, barred by his English-Irish heritage.

While the legend of the mob persists to this day, the reality for those who lived the life is less glamorous. Jerry unveils the hard truth, stripping away the myth to reveal the harsh realities of organized crime.

This is one man's search for redemption from a life of bad choices.

Chapter 2 *Beginnings*

The Tillinghast name dates to at least the 1500s in England before coming to America. The most prominent Tillinghast was Pardon Tillinghast, born in Sussex, England in 1622 who settled in New England in 1645. He became a well-to-do merchant and the sixth pastor of The First Baptist Church in Providence. Founded by Roger Williams, Pardon was a close friend.

Pardon, like many men of his time, was a farmer and a preacher. At 21-years old, the Cambridge educated Pardon fled England to escape from King Charles, who demanded adherence to the High Anglican Church. It took two years before he settled in Rhode Island. By 1665, he had amassed 25 acres of farmland and built his first home on what is now the Providence River.

Pardon erected a meeting house for the First Baptist Church founded by Roger Williams, becoming the church's sixth pastor and serving until his death in 1718 at age 96.

Along the way, he had two wives who bore him twelve children. His family grew to include seventy-nine grandchildren. One great-grandson also bore the name, Pardon Tillinghast. Nicknamed 'Molasses,' he earned a fortune as a slave trader. His wealth permitted him to grant a farm and land to each of his nine children.

Through the years there have been thousands of Tillinghast

descendants including Julia Ward Howe, author of The Battle Hymn of the Republic and Stephen Douglas who gained fame by debating and defeating U.S. Senate candidate Abraham Lincoln.

Lincoln himself is connected to the Tillinghast family through his association with Obadiah Holmes, a Baptist minister in Newport. Holmes married one of Pardon's granddaughters.

Pardon Elisha Tillinghast (1836-1905) served as a Justice on the Rhode Island Supreme Court, rising to Chief Justice in 1904, and served until his death.

The Tillinghasts were a patriotic family, serving in the Revolutionary and Civil Wars. They were lawyers, civil servants, and educators. Several became trustees at Brown University. The influence and legacy of this branch of the Tillinghast family are still evident at the Tillinghast Pond Management Area in West Greenwich, Rhode Island. A state park containing hundreds of acres of pristine woodland surrounding Tillinghast Pond. Remnants of old colonial-era buildings, historical grave markers hidden in the woods, and plentiful native wildlife fill the area.

The contrast to the legacy of the more modern-day generation of the Tillinghast name could not be more dramatic.

The Tillinghast Clan of South Providence

Gerald Martin 'Jerry' Tillinghast was born March 11, 1946, sharing the same birthday as his brother, Harold, three years older. He was the fourth son of John Charles Brown Tillinghast Sr., from Harmony, Rhode Island and second son of Helen (Maitland) Tillinghast from Brooklyn, New York.

Jerry comes from a large, diverse family. John C. Tillinghast and William Tillinghast are his older half-brothers. Harold was born in 1943, followed by Jerry in 1946. The family continued to grow with the additions of John Charles Brown Tillinghast Jr., who they called Junie, Helen (Sissy), and then Robert. Larry and Joanne, also half-brother and sister followed, although the family considered themselves all the same.

Jerry's branch of the Tillinghast family tree took root as a south Providence family. Their father worked as a stone mason, often traveling to work sites away from home for days at a time. When Jerry and Harold were older, they sometimes accompanied their father. Building themselves physically through hard work. By the time they were approaching their teens, their reputations for toughness and strength had grown.

Jerry recalls getting into a fight every day as he made his way to school from the Roger Williams Housing Project where the Tillinghasts lived. Built during World War II, the apartments would lure black families from other parts of the city with affordable housing changing the majority makeup of the area over time. It was tenement living, with absentee landlords, but pleasant enough.

"I got tired of fighting every day, so I figured if I beat them bad enough they'd leave me alone. Once I learned to fight by getting banged around by my brothers, it worked."

Jerry and Harold both attended Catholic school under the strict and watchful eyes of nuns. Their careers as Catholic school students (Jerry was a choir and altar boy) came to a sudden end the day Harold, then in the seventh grade, asked to go to the bathroom.

The nun teaching the class said no. Jerry laughed as he recalled the day.

"He said if he couldn't go, he would shit in the wastepaper basket. The good sister still said no. So, he walked over to the basket, pulled his pants down and shit in it. The nun slapped him in

9

the face. When he got home, my mother wanted to know what happened to his face. I said the nun slapped him because he did something bad. I never saw my mother's face get so drained."

The following morning Jerry and Harold walked to school with their mother who confronted the nun.

"My mother slapped her right in the mouth. It spun her around, twisting her habit sideways, and knocked her on the ass. I figured we're never gonna get to heaven now."

From that day forward, until the boys dropped out, it was public school education.

Following in the footsteps of his brother Harold, Jerry quit school after the ninth grade to work with his father, learning the stone mason trade. It was a much more productive life for the brothers, both expelled from more than one school for fighting. The work was hard physical labor building the physique that would come to terrorize others.

When did the world of crime raise its ugly head and take aim at the Tillinghast clan? It wasn't something planned. It was the environment in which they lived, and the crowd they hung with. As for Jerry, some of it might have been his experience in Vietnam as a United States Marine, a story that will unfold later. Whatever the reasons, it was a crowd and an atmosphere with prison as a likely destination.

"We had forty or fifty of us," remembered Jerry. "We ran in a crowd. Back then there was a lot of peer pressure. We stole a few cars. The first time I got arrested I was about fifteen. We were over at Hartford Avenue throwing rocks at animals. Across the way, some other kids were throwing rocks at cars. We got arrested even though we were nowhere near the kids who were throwing rocks at cars. We got put on probation. I told the probation officer I wasn't coming back for something I didn't do."

Jerry and his friends would expand their opportunities for mischief by exploring, and exploiting local businesses.

The Tip Top Bakery was a landmark in Providence for many years. Located on Globe Street, called the Ward Baking Company with locations all over the United States, Tip Top Bread and, later, Hostess Cupcakes, made the company a household name. It was an attractive location for young, hungry, and unrestrained Jerry and friends.

Each day the workers put fresh bread on a platform for the trucks to pick up and deliver. The memory of the aroma of fresh bread and the quick score brings a smile to Jerry's face.

"There was about thirty of us, and we'd go down to the bakery where they put out the fresh bread. Some of us would distract the staff while the rest of us would steal the stuff. The company also had a sort of thrift shop where they would sell day-old donuts and bread. One Saturday morning the manager comes out and says they were going to leave some day-old stuff for us, so we don't keep messing up the inventory for the trucks delivering the fresh stuff. One day, a new manager comes out and says we're not getting any more. He says to get out of there before he kicks our asses. Imagine, there were about thirty-five of us. So, we rifled the thrift store."

Jerry and his brothers were a tight-knit group despite getting into trouble so often. They were not bullying, neither were they bullied by other boys because of this bond.

When Jerry was 15, he was friendly with a boy named Jackie Melvin whose older brother, Raymond, was a bully.

"He used to come around us younger guys when we were playing football in the yard at Friendship Street School," remembers Jerry. "He'd grab the ball and run over everybody because he was bigger than us,"

"He played dirty football, he'd knee you and stuff. I told Jackie that if Raymond came up the middle in the game and tries anything, I'm punching him right in the fucking mouth."

It didn't take long for Raymond to try. He came dashing up the middle trying to knee Jerry in the balls.

"I said, 'Hey Raymond, this is a friendly football game.' Then, I punched him right in the mouth. Knocked him flat on his ass. I jumped on him and wailed the shit out of him. Everyone was dumbfounded because he was one of the tough guys in the neighborhood. From that day on he never bothered us and really never came around."

Another time, Jerry confronted two other guys who he called the "B" brothers. They were known for ganging up and beating on kids. On the day Jerry got into an argument with them, he beat them both. Despite the beating, they remained friends.

Jerry still contends he didn't look for trouble.

One of Jerry's granddaughters enlisted in the military. He attended a going away party for her. During a Karaoke sing, one of those "B" brothers was on stage. It was the first time Jerry had seen him in many years. During a break, Jerry followed him outside, staring at him.

The brother said, 'do I know you"?

"Yes, you do."

When the 'B' brother recognized Jerry, he chuckled. 'How could I forget the guy who beat up my brother and me at the same time?'

Jerry's brothers, John, Harold, and Billy were all fighters and worked out in the basement of their home. They also worked on their defensive moves and always agreed to stick together no matter what. They taught Jerry to fight and instilled a sense of toughness and a drive to never back down.

It was both a blessing and a curse.

Jerry's path to a reputation for toughness and ignoring social norms continued through his youth.

When Jerry and his crowd were in their early teens, nothing was sacred. One of their south Providence black friends suggested having them put sheets over their heads and pretend to be KKK members beating him up.

As darkness settled in the boys put on the sheets with cutouts for their eyes and attacked their willing cohort as he lay on the sidewalk in the city's south end. They were disappointed no one stopped, until a bus pulled up. A large black man got out and came running over, yelling at the sheet-wearing boys as they ran away.

The bus driver, still worried about the "victim," asked if he was okay. The kid laughed as he explained they were only playing. This enraged the bus driver and, according to Jerry, "he beat the shit out of the kid."

The opportunities for less sophomoric, more criminal behavior, soon drew their attention.

Imperial Knife, a long-time landmark company in Providence, was one of the most successful businesses in Rhode Island. The company started as Empire Knife in Winsted, Connecticut, then moved to Providence in 1916 to be close to the jewelry district. It grew to become the largest maker of knives in the United States. To the crooks and wannabe crooks, it was reputed to be burglar-proof.

The word was out that no one could ever break into Imperial Knife.

One of Jerry's first cousins said he had figured out a way into Imperial Knife. Jerry did not believe him. The teenagers made their way to a spot in the rear of the building and got in. Jerry remembered a low window as the entry point. Inside they saw knives everywhere, all shapes and sizes.

"We got sturdy bags and filled them up. My brothers took the bigger knives. They told us we shouldn't be stealing those things anyway. They shook us down for the better ones by threatening to rat us out."

Jerry and his cousin never returned to Imperial Knife. Despite having lots of knives to hand out to friends, they never admitted to stealing them either. It was always, "we found them."

Jerry's young 'playmates' numbered about fifty. Today they'd be called a gang. One summer they watched the progress of construction on the new Blackstone Street school, close to Jerry's house. It was not a welcome addition to the neighborhood. They preferred to bunk school. This would make it harder. In their young minds, breaking the windows would derail the new school.

"We figured they would forget about building the school if we kept breaking all the windows. That's how stupid we were."

One day, a large school bus pulled up to the construction site, and two Providence police officers got out. They ordered the kids to get on-board.

"They came to each house, talked to our parents, and told them they were taking all the kids in that neighborhood to a police camp in Galilee. There were two options: Go there for two weeks until they finished the school or face jail.

Jerry never thought for a minute his parents would send him to the camp, but they did. To his surprise, he enjoyed the two weeks and wound up staying; camping in the woods and enjoying the outdoors, despite the close supervision.

One counselor and Jerry locked horns. During a family visit, Jerry told his brothers Billy and John about the counselor giving him a hard time.

14

"They kicked the shit out him. He was all bloody. I said 'whoa, you're gonna kill him.'"

Despite the altercation, Jerry stayed at the camp through the summer. He recalled there was a girl's camp nearby, and the boys tried to sneak off. The girls did the same thing, but the counselors were sharp.

"They watched our barracks like hawks. We were bad, troublemakers."

Back at home, things fell into a familiar pattern, time moved on, and Jerry entered his middle-teen years.

15-year-old boys could get in a lot of trouble in South Providence, Rhode Island in the 1960s. More so when the father of one of them owned a garage and didn't pay attention to how it was being used.

Bicycle theft is a common problem, but Jerry and friends took it to a new level. It was Jerry's first experience with 'organized' crime. There was never a shortage of bikes to swipe, repaint, and sell to an unsuspecting public.

"We stole bikes all over the state. Kids would take a bus somewhere, get a bike, and ride it back to the garage. We would hoist the bike up on ceiling hooks, change identifying numbers, then we'd paint them and sell them."

Parents, not so innocently blind to the operation, would come to the garage to buy the bikes, figuring it was a lot cheaper than going to a store.

"It was pretty good for a while, but it ended when the kid's father who owned the garage found out about it. He closed the garage and used it for his truck and car. He couldn't figure out where all the bikes came from. There were seats and handlebars and other bike parts everywhere. That was the end of that."

Then there was the Granny Caper.

Jerry's grandmother, Gertrude Maitland, was legally blind. She often relied on him to take her home after visiting her daughter, Helen, Jerry' mother. She used a walker, so family members took turns driving her home.

He was at a bowling alley in Cranston playing pool, a place that would play a decisive role in Jerry's future, when he realized he had to take her home. "I didn't have a car then," Jerry said, "so I told my friend we had to grab one."

Parked nearby was a '53 Chevy with the key in the ignition.

"It had one of those ignitions where you could turn it and pull the key out, and it didn't really lock. We could hot-wire it anyway. You take the silver paper from a bubble gum wrapper, pull the wires out behind the ignition, out the silver paper on the three little prongs and start the car."

They drove to Jerry's house where he told his friend to drive his grandmother home. The friend protested saying he didn't want to drive a stolen car.

"She don't know that and can't see anyway. Tell her your name is Bob," Jerry said.

"What if a cop stops the car?" the friend asked.

"Leave her there. Get out and run," Jerry told him. "The cops aren't going to arrest her."

Such a cavalier attitude to stealing cars was a preview of things to come. Each new episode served as a building block in Jerry's street education.

Another day in the young life of Jerry and his pals.

The crowd Jerry ran with didn't limit themselves to just one area of the city. They ventured out, expanding their opportunities for petty crime and profit.

Although they were from South Providence, they hung out in other areas of the city, one of their favorites was Fox Point.

16

Home to a large Portuguese population, it was once a major seaport and one of the oldest neighborhoods in the city with settlers arriving with Roger Williams in the 1600s. Although those first colonists were farmers, by 1680 the area became a focal point for shipping with vessels trading with the West Indies. They named a large section of Fox Point along the waterfront India Point after "India men" and the ships they sailed carrying out their trade.

In the middle of the 18th century, Cape Verdeans and Azoreans immigrated in search of jobs on the waterfront and in the many factories which flourished. They also built Catholic churches which stand today.

Fox Point differed from South Providence, just a few miles away. Jerry's home in the government-built Roger Williams Housing Project contrasted with the tenement houses of Fox Point.

The opportunity for cross-cultural experiences was different in the 50s and 60s. People stayed within their own, more homogenous, neighborhoods

Federal Hill was predominately Italian, Southside post-World War II tended to be English/Irish Catholic, morphing to a majority of black families, and Fox Point housed Portuguese and Cape Verdean immigrants.

Most of the time, Jerry and his friends would hang around their own neighborhoods of south Providence. One of their favorite spots was in front of Tommy Webster's house on Friendship Street, one of the oldest recorded streets in the city.

"At any given time, you might find thirty or forty kids there. One hot summer day, a cop pulls up on a motorcycle. There were about seventy-five of us then, and he says this is his beat now and if he found out anyone was doing something wrong, he was gonna kick their asses. The next thing I knew he was off his motorcycle, stripped of his clothes, beat up and his gun taken. It was a tough environment."

Jerry was about sixteen when he had his first encounter with a junkie. It occurred in the attic of Jerry's house.

The junkie was a friend of one of his brothers. He asked Jerry to help him shoot up, which horrified Jerry. He described the incident to his brothers.

"My brother Billy beat the dog shit out of the guy."

It made a lasting impression in young Jerry. He avoided the lure of drugs many of his friends, and some of his family, did not.

"We'd go out, get drunk, and still be home by 10, or my father would be out hunting me down."

Today, as Jerry and some of those boyhood friends reach old age, the friendships endure. They know of his past; the allegations he beat, the ones that stuck, and the jail time he served.

Yet most remain loyal.

Thomas Hartley, also known as 'Red Ball,' so named by crime boss Patriarca, has a violent criminal past. He cannot associate with Jerry or any other felon without approval by the parole board. He says he's always loved Jerry, and they used to joke about who was better looking. Hartley claims the only person tougher than Jerry was Jerry's second wife, Terry.

"He never looked for trouble," Hartley recalled, "but he was a tough kid and could handle himself."

Hartley once served an eight-year prison term for conspiracy to commit arson. Like Jerry, Hartley says the hardest part of prison is leaving family behind on visiting day and holidays.

Hartley is several years older than Jerry and was friends with his brother John before Jerry was even born. A close associate of many of the well-known mob members, Hartley's last arrest was at age 74.

In 2011, he and others mob figures, among them Frank

'Bobo' Marrapese, Edward Lato, and Alfred 'Chippy' Scivola, were arrested after a six-month State Police investigation into organized criminal gambling. Hartley pled nolo to several counts of conspiracy and received a 5-year suspended prison sentence.

The pattern of behavior, set deep in some, goes on. It was these early influences that drove many of Jerry's later choices.

Chapter 3 *A Call to Arms*

JFK and Enlisting in the Marine Corps

On November 22, 1963, the assassination of John Fitzgerald Kennedy, the 46-year-old President of the United States, shocked the world. It disturbed the impressionable Jerry.

"It affected me so bad, I wanted to get even with someone. Then I realized it was probably our own government that had taken out the President. I was 17 years old. I was just a kid, but I was smart enough to figure it out."

The world was changing, and Jerry stood at one of those crossroads of life.

Walking to his brother's house after learning of the President's assassination, a friend offered him a ride. In the car was a young girl. The friend said it was his uncle's car and the girl his cousin.

A police car came up behind them.

"The guy says, 'oh shit,' I stole this car, and she's a runaway from the training school.'"

Jerry wanted to strangle the guy, but with the police closing in made another choice. Not a well calculated one. He jumped from the moving car, slamming headfirst into a telephone pole.

He came to in jail.

Since he was the one adult in the car, the cops arraigned him on the charge of possession of a stolen auto and aiding an escape. They set his court date for March 31st. He needed a plan to avoid going to jail.

It was time for a decision. Eighteen-years-old, facing his first criminal charges as an adult, he looked for a way out of the jam.

His first choice was to visit a U.S. Army recruiting office. He asked if they could induct him before March 31st. The recruiter told him it would be a week after that. Another friend told Jerry he had just joined the Marines and bet Jerry $3.50 he didn't have the balls to enlist. The Marine recruiter said he could get Jerry in by March 31st, so he joined. Jerry spent $3.50 on cigarettes, although his friend never gave him the money.

In the hole on the wager, but escaping his court date, he was on his way to the United States Marine Corps Recruit Training Depot, Parris Island, South Carolina. His life as a Marine would take him to ambushes, booby-traps, and violent clashes with Viet Cong guerrillas in the hell of America's war in Vietnam.

The Marines would train him with the customary vigorous enthusiasm. Vietnam would teach him to survive and to kill. The Marine doctrine on unquestioning adherence to orders would put him in the crosshairs of the politics of that war and earn him his first stint in prison.

The Marine Corps Parris Island

In their first few moments at the United States Marine Corps Recruit Training Depot at Parris Island, every recruit has one common thought.

"What the hell have I done?"

The drill instructors storm the bus, and the nightmare begins. Organized chaos engulfs the recruits, designed to disorient those who would become Marines, disabusing them of any preconceived confidences or certainties.

The recruits get one thing handed to them; an opportunity to become Marines. Everything else they would have to earn. For Jerry Tillinghast, his first few moments were like everyone else, but his toughness gained on the streets of Providence overcame his fear. Certain as anyone could be amid the nightmarish world of Marine Corps boot camp, he knew he would survive and become a United States Marine.

Thirteen weeks later, having completed the grueling training, Jerry held the globe and anchor symbol of the Marines in his hand. The drill instructors did their job; Jerry was now a Marine.

Boot camp stripped away the civilian, instilled discipline, toughened his body, and taught him the skills of a combat infantryman. The Viet Cong and the contradictions of the war would strip him of his conscience.

The Marine Corps would teach him how to kill. Vietnam would make him good at it and immunize him to the inhumanity of taking a human life.

It is how combat works. First, you train skills, then you dehumanize the enemy. Killing Nguyen or Thieu is hard. Killing a gook, or slope, or dink is easy.

Jerry arrived in Parris Island and began his recruit training on April 1, 1964, completing boot camp on June 25, 1964. After boot camp, they sent Jerry to advanced infantry training then assigned him to various Marine operations. He served in Norway and the Dominican Republic. The first of what would be several controversial incursions by American military into local affairs.

On his return from these assignments, while stationed at Quantico Marine Base as a rifle instructor, he requested a transfer to Marine Reconnaissance Training. His commanding officer (CO) turned down the request, so Jerry volunteered for Vietnam. The CO granted this one.

Next Stop: Vietnam

The first American combat troops arrived in Vietnam in 1965. General William Westmoreland, Commanding General of MAC-V, Military Assistance Command-Vietnam, ordered the Marines sent in-country to defend the airbases used in the bombing campaign over North Vietnam. Westmoreland's strategy morphed from the small, strategic targeting of the Viet Cong infrastructure that the Marines favored and executed with extraordinary success, into a massive search and destroy mission with overwhelming firepower and extensive use of artillery and air power.

Jerry would be part of this new battle plan to 'win' the war. He and his fellow Marines would be the cannon fodder for what would prove, in the long run, to be a military victory tarnished by false measures of success and tainted by political defeat.

The cost of the American military victory in Vietnam destroyed the fabric of American society.

Chapter 4   *Welcome to Hell*

"Abandon all hope, ye who enter here."
                              Dante Alighieri 'Inferno'

Arriving in Chu Lai Vietnam in 1966, Jerry's orders sent him to Company "A" 1st Bn/7th Regiment/1st Marine Division. In his service record, there are two significant operations listed; Operation Nevada/Lien Ket 34 and Operation Montgomery/Lien Ket 40. Both were search and destroy missions focused on hardcore Viet Cong units operating in the Ba Lang An Peninsula, thirty-two kilometers south of Chu Lai Quang Ngai Province. The peninsula was a Viet Cong stronghold with considerable support from the local villagers. In 1965, the first regimental size battle of just American forces operating in combat took place here.

This area of Vietnam was the scene of many American casualties, much heroism, and immense tragedies. One of the most tragic incidents happened at the nearby village of My Lai.

In March 1969 a patrol from the U.S. Army 23rd (Americal) Infantry Division under the command of Lt. William Calley, Jr., executed between 300-500 unarmed civilians—men, women, and children—in the village of Son My. It became known as the My Lai Massacre in the U.S. and the Son My Massacre in Vietnam.

By the time Jerry arrived in-country, Westmoreland's search and destroy tactics were in place throughout the American theater of operation. Marine and U.S. Army patrols would encircle a village,

24

then enter and search for any known or suspected Viet Cong, supporters, supplies, or weapons. Intelligence units, later formalized into Project Phoenix, would provide lists of known or suspected Viet Cong to the squad leaders. They would use these lists to locate and apprehend, if possible, or kill the Viet Cong fighters.

Language, cultural differences, and the increasing local support of the Viet Cong due to the oppressive actions of the South Vietnamese government and the collateral damage from the destructive force of the American military led to tense and dangerous conditions for Marine patrols on the ground.

Jerry took part in two division-size search and destroy missions. He saw heavy Marine and South Vietnamese Army casualties, with several Marines killed in action. Viet Cong losses, according to the archived situation reports, were high. However, since the end of the war, many of the original combat reports are now considered highly inaccurate.

One of the most tragic results of Westmoreland's reliance on body counts as indications of success against the enemy became a classic case of the tail wagging the dog.

For example, during one patrol near a suspected VC controlled village, Marines engaged elements of the local Viet Cong. They reported killing six confirmed and three suspected VC guerrillas and recovering one weapon. This questionable body-to-weapon ratio resulted from the increased demand for field results. The expectations of MAC-V, the Military Assistance Command-Vietnam, tacitly encouraged inflated reporting. In the rice patties, mountains, and jungles of Vietnam, if you found two hands, they counted it as two dead enemy combatants.

Three fingers, a hat-trick. Ten fingers, a gold mine.

The focus on numbers proved misleading. In a war with no

defined lines of engagement and an elusive enemy who could vanish into tunnels or blend in with the local population, success was difficult to measure. Such intangibility compounded the anger visited on local villagers suspected of aiding the VC.

Marines took casualties, losing fellow Marines to Viet Cong booby-traps and attacks, and faced an uncooperative and often hostile local population. All the ingredients for vengeful retaliation existed as these patrols of young men—18,19, and 20-years old-passed through now quiet villages where once the Marines received intense fire.

They would repeat the process, often at the same village, over and over with no demonstrable sense of gaining any meaningful measure of success. Losing fellow Marines, bonds forged in the furnace of combat, over and over again.

During a patrol in the hamlet of Song Tra II, the emotions, tension, and anger reached the boiling point.

Jerry recalls the day.

"It was, I believe, in the morning. Our squad was on patrol when we walked into a hamlet that was supposed to be infested by the Viet Cong. As we approached this hamlet, we stopped and were briefed by our squad leader, Corporal Williams, on what was supposed to be very accurate information about the goings-on in the village. The corporal said to do what was a routine practice and select a villager to put at the front of the squad as if there was any VC or booby-traps, the villagers always knew and would say so. They would say 'number ten or number one. Ten was bad, one was good. Nothing ever in between. They'd get nervous if we got close to a booby trap, 'number ten, number ten' they'd yell and point it out.

"We did it every time we went in. If we wanted to fill the canteens at the well, we'd make them drink it first. The VC would poison the well if the villagers weren't cooperating. The VC were brutal to their own people. It was hard to see all this. Especially the kids. I got along with them. I'd teach them songs to sing. The little ones didn't understand what was going on.

"You had to be careful, though. In the hamlets and villages where the VC were active, they'd use kids, 5 or 6-years old, to roll grenades into a patrol or detonate a bomb. The VC were smart, they'd make booby-traps out of all sorts of things. They'd set 'em up so it wouldn't take out the first guy, they wanted to get the ones in the middle. Create confusion. Sometimes it was designed to wound a Marine, not kill them. They knew we never left anyone behind. The wounded would slow us down, and they'd try to pick us all off. Or they might get a medevac chopper when it came in to rescue the wounded.

Jerry looked off into space as the memories rushed back. "They couldn't take us on head-to-head. We'd wipe 'em out. A Marine rifle platoon with a couple of machine guns, that's what I did, hump the machine gun, was a powerful force. They couldn't take us on directly, so they did what they could; snipers, booby-traps that sort of thing."

Tactics, strategy, political realities are meaningless to those immersed in combat. These were 18, 19, 20-year-old kids full of brawn and balls. Fear, terror, or tears were something you kept buried deep. You only let them out in those dark, lonely moments of solitude in a pitch-black night while a silent enemy wandered mere feet away, nursing his own fears.

Jerry's unit entered the hamlet of Song Tra II. The Marine on point was Corporal Williams. He grabbed a woman, because she had no ID card, and put her at the head of the column.

"The officers and NCOs never told us much. They'd just send us in and have us bring the villagers to them to check against the list. Anyone without an ID card was suspect."

"Sometimes," Jerry recalled, "when we'd go into a village, you'd hear a bell ring. We figured out it was someone counting the Marines to let the VC know how many of us there were. We had to use the villagers to protect ourselves.

"We then proceeded through the village searching for the VC. The Corporal had a list. I think either the woman he grabbed or her husband was on the list of suspected VCs. I don't know, but they never told us much anyway other than what to do. At the other end of the village, we came to a small body of water. The corporal told us to set up a 360-degree perimeter to protect all our flanks. The area wasn't large enough to do that, so we set up a 280-degree perimeter which was good enough for our position.

"I was a Lance Corporal in charge of the machine gun team with two team assistants/ammo carriers. We asked the corporal, who was black, what we were going to do now that we could find no VC. There was a lot of tension between black and white Marines. Either the Vietnamese Regular Hard Core or the Red Chinese Army were all through Vietnam spreading fliers with words such as 'all our black brothers kill your white counterparts' and join us. It was done to cause friction among our rank and file, and to some degree it did. Based on the fact that some black Marines were playing around with the idea of doing what the fliers said, I would have the black Marines walk in front of me 90% of the time.

"One of the black Marines named Spencer, who would be a star witness against me at my trial, walked in front of me at all times. I was 19 or 20 years old and scared enough fighting for my life and country without taking the chance that a fellow Marine would want to shoot me in the back and try to make it look like an accident.

"At the time we set up our perimeter, the corporal took the

woman and put her at the head of the squad and made her sit down at the base of a tree. Some of us were trying to scare her into telling us if she knew about any Cong in the area. She kept saying no, and I dropped my bayonet at her feet to frighten her into telling us what she knew. Then the corporal came over and grabbed her saying he had enough of this shit and ordered a Marine to tie her up because he was going to fuck her. We didn't think he was going to do it. We thought he was just trying to scare her into telling us if she knew anything. The corporal said he was serious. Caldwell, not having any rope, pulled her pants off and used them to tie her up saying he was going to go next. The rest of us didn't know how to act in such a situation. Everything happened so fast, within 30 seconds Corporal Williams had his pants down and was on top of her. A few minutes later, Caldwell was raping her. While this was going on, I was asked if I was going to go next and I said are you crazy. I wouldn't fuck her with your dick. The other guys were milling around, but no one did anything to stop them. After they were through, Williams ordered me to untie her. I asked him why me? He said because I told you to. I took that as an order. It was driven into our brains at boot camp that to refuse an order in battle could get you shot for cowardice, so I took off her blindfold. I was the last one she saw.

"The corporal had us pack up our gear, and we left. No one said a word. Most of us were pissed but still stayed quiet about the situation until later that evening when there was a big commotion. The whole camp came out of their tents to see what was going on. We soon found out that a bunch of Vietnamese women was saying someone raped their friend. They were yelling and very pissed off and rightly so.

"After a short while, things seemed to calm down. Someone entered my tent and said my presence was required at the CO's

29

tent. Inside, with the CO, was another high-ranking officer. He told me to sit down and go over the entire day's activities, which I did. When asked what happened to the woman I said I didn't see anything.

"The woman had already been brought to camp. The CO had all the Marines who were out on that patrol line up so she could pick out those who raped her. She then picked out Williams, Caldwell and me from that lineup."

A Miscarriage of Justice

Within a few weeks, Jerry's world moved from the dangerous enemy-filled rice paddies and the uncertainties of combat into the confusing nightmare of a court-martial.

1st Lieutenant Daniel Hanlon represented Jerry at the court-martial. In the world of the Judge Advocate General, lawyers are interchangeable. One case they are assigned as prosecutors, the next as defense counsel. Like any court environment, and more so in the insular world of the military, familiarity and shared experiences often count more than justice.

Hanlon, who would go on to a long and distinguished career in California rising to become the Presiding Judge of the San Francisco Superior Court and culminating with his serving as Presiding Justice of the California Court of Appeal. In his fifty-plus year legal career, just a few cases stood out as genuine miscarriages of justice.

The case involving Lance Corporal Gerald M. 'Jerry' Tillinghast was one.

The JAG office assigned Lieutenant Hanlon as defense counsel for Jerry on 23 July 1966. This was his ninth general court-martial. He came to division legal in early June; until then he had been with the 5th Marines as legal counsel to Brig. Gen. Chuck Widecke, and acting XO of Headquarters Company, 5th Marines.

By the time he left Vietnam in February of 1967, Hanlon had tried thirty-six general court-martial cases

The relationship of the captain with the senior officer on the panel hearing the cases troubled Hanlon. The captain represented Corporal Williams, who was in charge of the squad and the first of the two Marines to rape the woman,

Based on the testimony of the victim and several fellow Marines, the court-martial panel found Jerry guilty of aiding and abetting the crime of rape. They convicted Williams, the corporal who had ordered the woman tied up, and Caldwell, the private who had pulled off the woman's pants to use as a blindfold on the woman, of rape.

In the closing arguments Jerry's JAG lawyer, Lieutenant Hanlon, argued that the evidence did not support the charge.

Hanlon restated the facts as provided in the testimony of several Marines in the patrol. Corporal Williams, a highly regarded and respected squad leader who'd been recommended for meritorious promotion to sergeant, was upset by an incident the previous evening.

Williams felt he had let down the squad.

During a night ambush position, Williams had ordered the squad into a fifty percent alert. Half the Marines slept while half remained on alert. Williams found out in the morning that while he slept, the alert Marines had watched as fifteen armed Viet Cong slipped past their ambush, never engaging the enemy.

Williams reported this to the CO (Company commander) and was informed there would be further action once the CO reviewed the reports. Williams was angry with himself and with the Marines who had failed to follow his directives. This set the stage for the incident in the village of Song Tra.

While some of the squad went to check activity near some boats on the shore, Jerry set up his machine gun position and guarded the woman. While she was there, the Marines taunted her. Jerry admitted to brandishing a bayonet and tossing it at the woman's feet.

"It's something we did with VC suspects, I never believed for one second it was anything more than intimidation. Just trying to get information and save Marine lives.

"She wasn't a scared woman to us, she was the enemy until we found out otherwise. It's the way it was."

After returning from the beach, Williams ordered the woman to be tied up. Caldwell stripped off the woman's pants and used them to tie her hands and cover her eyes. Jerry asked Williams what they would do with the woman.

When the Corporal got on top of the woman, Jerry and the other Marine were at a loss for what to do. They didn't know if the woman chose to go along with it to get let go or to get something from the Marines.

It was a no-win situation. Yet, when it was all said and done, the Marine Corps charged only three Marines; Williams, Caldwell, and Jerry. No other members of the squad faced charges despite each of them being there for the entire episode.

Hanlon argued that up to the moment the Corporal assaulted the woman, Jerry had no way of knowing what the Corporal intended. His actions were not that of someone aiding and abetting a rape, but of a young Marine trying to keep himself and his fellow Marines alive.

The woman was a potential enemy and a source of valuable information. They repeated similar actions throughout Vietnam in the villages, hamlets, and paddies infiltrated by the Viet Cong.

Hanlon argued that the woman testified Jerry did not rape her but merely untied her at the Corporal's orders. She never testified about the bayonet or any of the other actions of the other Marines. Yet, of all the other squad members present during the incident, Jerry was the only Marine charged as an accessory. The case was a manifest miscarriage of justice.

The argument fell on deaf ears.

Court-Martial

The official transcript of the court-martial is rife with errors of fact. The members of the board sitting in judgment could not keep the story straight. In one summary, they had Jerry tying the woman's hand. This was in direct conflict with the trial testimony of witnesses and statements by his co-defendants.

In a second summary, written to deny Jerry's appeal they specifically mentioned Jerry walked away once the rape began, never touching the woman until Williams ordered him to take off her blindfold and untie her. The record includes testimony from Lance Corporal Spencer who ordered the Marines, including Jerry, away from the woman until Williams decided otherwise. This hearing officer also detailed how the entire squad of Marines stood around while the rape occurred.

The government gave no reason for not charging other Marines. The decision goes a step further in saying, "the record is not clear whether the accused blindfolded (the victim) as an original thought or at the prompting of others." The victim herself testified that Jerry never touched her except to untie her. Such contradicting evidence is then the basis on which the board convicted Jerry.

The decision astounded Jerry's defense counsel.

Williams, the squad leader and first to rape the woman, received a five-year sentence, reduction and rank, and Bad Conduct Discharge.

Underscoring the racial misconceptions of the time, Williams lawyer argued the corporal's race played a factor in his actions. They used the stereotype of hyper-sexuality by black men, negroes in the language of the time, in their argument for leniency. The appellate panel reduced Williams' time to serve to two years.

Caldwell, who also raped the woman, received ten months to serve, reduction in rank, forfeit all pay and benefits, and a Bad Conduct Discharge.

They sentenced Jerry to a reduction in rank from Lance Corporal to Private, forfeit of all pay and benefits, confined to Portsmouth Naval Prison for one year, and given a dishonorable discharge.

The disparities in the sentences imposed shocked Jerry's lawyer. Hanlon believed the case against Jerry was just to appease the angry Vietnamese villagers. They used him as a pawn in a complex political struggle to gain the support of the local Vietnamese people.

To support his position, Hanlon cited the differences in the sentence length and the discharge type. There is a significant difference between a Bad Conduct Discharge and a Dishonorable Discharge.

Unlike an administrative discharge, a Bad Conduct Discharge (BCD) is a punitive discharge that can only be given by a court-martial (either Special or General) as punishment to an enlisted service-member. Bad conduct discharges are often preceded by a period of confinement in a military prison. The discharge itself is not executed until completion of both confinement and the appellate review process. Virtually all veterans' benefits are forfeited by a Bad Conduct Discharge. In the language of vets, it is also referred to as the "Big Chicken Dinner."

A dishonorable discharge (DD), like a BCD, is a punitive discharge rather than an administrative discharge. It can only be handed down to an enlisted member by a general court-martial. Dishonorable discharges are handed down for what the military considers the most reprehensible conduct. This type of discharge may be rendered only by conviction at a general court-martial for serious offenses (e.g., desertion, sexual assault, murder, etc.) that call for dishonorable discharge as part of the sentence. With this characterization of service, all veterans' benefits are lost, regardless of any past honorable service.

This type of discharge is universally regarded as shameful, and the social stigma attached to it makes it very difficult to obtain gainful post-service employment. Additionally, U.S. federal law prohibits ownership of firearms by those who have been dishonorably discharged. [2] In most cases, a person who receives a dishonorable discharge loses the right to vote and the right to receive government assistance of any kind. They cannot obtain a bank loan, and they are unable to find work at the state or government level. Finding gainful civilian employment is also an arduous task for someone with a DD as most states now require employers to conduct background checks and the results of military records and discharges are often disclosed. Going to college is another pitfall because government loans and grants are unavailable for anyone with a DD. This is a permanent record that will follow the individual for the duration of their lives anywhere in the world. In some U.S. states, the United Kingdom and other countries this may be for the duration of his/her sentence, elsewhere this may be permanent.[1]

In his appeal, Jerry's JAG lawyer argued that the verdict was in conflict with the testimony of the victim herself. She testified that Jerry did not take part in the rape. She picked him out as the Marine who untied her. They charged none of the other Marines present at the scene. Several of the Marine witnesses had as much involvement in the incident as Jerry, yet no other member of the squad was charged with any crimes. Jerry's actions at the time were because of an order by a superior officer, not evidence of voluntary participation.

Jerry's actions in tossing the bayonet at the woman's feet were nothing out of the ordinary for treatment of suspected enemy combatants. This was a military operation, in enemy-controlled territory, and reflected standard operating protocols. While such actions, viewed in the antiseptic environment of a courtroom, may appear reprehensible, they were considered necessary and useful in saving American lives in the dangerous villages and rice paddies of Vietnam.

Jerry's lawyer argued that under the rigid structure of the Marine Corps, particularly while in combat, the order of a superior must be obeyed without question. The Corporal never ordered Jerry to rape the woman. That would have been an unlawful order. Instead, he ordered Jerry to untie her and remove her blindfold.

How, Jerry's lawyer argued, could anyone know that the Corporal and the other Marine intended to rape the woman?

---

[1] [From VOSB-Military-Discharge-Overview.pdf

https://www.vetverify.org]

Callous as it may sound, those young Marines faced an impossible situation. Why was Jerry, of all the other squad members, the only one charged?

The lawyer presented character witnesses as to Jerry's performance under fire and as a Marine machine gun squad leader. His fellow Marines characterized him as a capable, courageous, and conscientious Marine.

The record of testimony in the case shows that Corporal Charles Alexander, USMC, testified Jerry was "an outstanding Marine. Got along well with the kids in the villages and hamlets" of Vietnam.

"Lance Corporal Tillinghast was quick to volunteer for dangerous assignments, performed well under fire, and was an excellent machine gun squad leader."

The review board reduced Jerry's discharge conditions to a Bad Conduct Discharge but upheld the one-year sentence. In the face of the miscarriage of justice, Jerry's lawyer told him he was a scapegoat for the flawed policies of the military.

A later review by Chief Petty Officer J.L. Bradford, USN, and Lieutenant (j.g.) J.V. Connor, USN, Prison Personnel Officers, reported;

"Recommended on review that Private Tillinghast should not have been charged in this case and the record clearly reflected he did not participate in the rape."

They argued, *"The treatment of the woman in the field up to the time of the incident as a possible Viet Cong suspect or collaborator was consistent with normal operating protocols."*[2]

The reviewers recommended the bad conduct discharge be

---

[2] [Record Portsmouth Naval Prison files

suspended and Jerry reinstated to duty.

The appeal fell on deaf ears.

Jerry did his time, received a bad conduct discharge, and returned to the streets of Providence. He was bitter, angry, and indifferent to the rest of the world. The first in a series of bad choices charted a course.

"When I was being questioned, I would not cooperate with the process. I was brought up in a ghetto. To rat on someone was breaking a cardinal rule. I would have been blackballed with friends and family. It was my immature thinking at the time. I was sorry I didn't cooperate; however, I just couldn't bring myself to rat on Williams and Caldwell. If I had to do it all again, I would have spoken my peace. I got screwed for keeping my mouth shut. Williams admitted he raped her because of his culture. He said it is a sexual culture, so he got off and, I heard, was sent back to duty. I don't understand that.

"At the trial, when the woman was put on the stand, she was asked to point me out. She said I did not rape her, and that was why she picked me out of the lineup. I was found guilty. I was given a one-year sentence and a dishonorable discharge from the Marine Corps.

"My JAG lawyer was distraught over the verdict. Not knowing the military justice system, I asked what just happened to me. He said they made me a pawn and victim. He told me Caldwell's lawyer was a captain with considerable power and influence with the whole JAG command staff, including the colonel who presided over my court-martial. Maybe I was, or maybe I wasn't used as a pawn. But I know this much, I was victimized. To this day I believe I was used as a bargaining chip to satisfy the Vietnamese people. I was used as a political advancement for someone looking to advance through the ranks of JAG. I am truly sorry for thinking that

38

way, but it is what it is. I tried to talk to the captain for Caldwell, but I never got a response. I wanted to know what happened and how it happened. I was told by a clerk of the court not to try to contact the captain or anyone else involved in the trial process. My answer was... why not? You can't do anything more to me than what was already done. The clerk just walked away leaving me complaining to no avail. I just shut up and ended up going to prison. When I came home, I was a very bitter young man and very anti-government for being used as a tool, which I truly believed I was at the time, to appease our fucking enemy. Shortly after that, I came to a conclusion just how politically corrupt our military leaders could be at the time of war where the power of politics outweighed the lives and concerns of our fighting men and women of all branches of our military.

"I would like to take this time to thank all of our politically motivated upper-class high-ranking officers who were in power and our JAG echelon back then in Da Nang, Vietnam for letting a serious wrong ruin the life of a fighting man and throwing it down the proverbial toilet. But just so you will hear and know, I am and will always be a loyal and faithful United States Marine, Viet Nam veteran, and citizen of this great and powerful country of the United States of America. I am still a very, very proud American. I am a patriot!"

When Jerry was released after serving his time at the Portsmouth (NH) Naval Prison, his father and a close friend, Jackie Melvin, drove to New Hampshire to get him.

It was 1967. Jerry had spent three years in the Marine Corps, saw intense combat in Vietnam, and served a year in prison at hard labor for a crime he didn't commit; more time than one of the actual perpetrators.

He was twenty-one-years-old.

39

For the next few years, the chip on his shoulder would grow. It would compel him to challenge anyone or anything that got in his way. He decided that no one would ever have control over him, or intimidate him, again. His mistrust of authority grew all-consuming. His fearlessness brought him to the attention of both cops and bad guys.

Jerry's choices paved the way back to prison.

Chapter 5 *The Mayor and the Mob*

Missed Opportunities

When Jerry was a child, he had to fight almost every day to keep his twenty-five cents milk money. He lived 100 yards from the school, and he didn't want to keep fighting to get to school. His mother told Jerry's older brothers about the problem. They took him into their basement to toughen him up.

"I thank them now because they taught me to get tough and stand up for myself."

Growing up with those brothers gave Jerry a sense of helping the underdog many times over his long life.

Jerry tried turning that toughness into a career as a professional boxer.

"When I got out of the service, my father opened a small restaurant called Jerry's Grill on Eddy Street near the Temple Street School. Willie Greene, from South Providence, was a professional boxer who rose to the top ranks of middleweights. He worked as a janitor for a nearby school. Willie frequented Jerry's Grill and became friendly with my father who would talk about my toughness."

Jerry, like most people, knew about Wild Willie Greene. On March 7, 1961, Greene fought Terry Downes for the World

Middleweight championship at Empire Wembley in London. Willie had been New England Middleweight champion and once ranked 7th in the world.

Willie invited Jerry to train with him as a light heavyweight in the 190-pound class. Many youngsters were familiar with the CYO gym on Point Street located over the fire station. Many of the toughest fighters to come out of Rhode Island worked out there. Leo Hunt ran the gym, described by Jerry as a great guy.

Willie watched Jerry work and decided he had an 'educated left.'

Usually, a new fighter would go three rounds, but Willie trained Jerry for ten rounds. His idea was the other youngsters would be finished after three and Jerry would still be fresh. Willie also advised Jerry to "eat, sleep and live" boxing.

But it wasn't to be.

Jerry was supposed to be up very early to run at Roger Williams Park. One night at 11 o'clock Jerry was leaving the El Rio lounge as Willie was coming in.

"Why you here?" Willie asked Jerry.

Jerry smiled, trying to charm Willie. "Just hanging with my friends."

"That ain't gonna help you in the ring," Willie said, unmoved by the smile. "You might be a tough guy out on the street, but boxing is different. There are smart guys in there who will take you apart, they don't care how tough you are."

Jerry shrugged. "I'll run, I'll work out. Don't worry Willie."

But it was just another bad choice.

That incident, the death of Willie's father, with whom Willie was close, and Jerry's continued scrapes in street fights, brought an end to what might have been a successful boxing career.

Willie, known as Eagle Heart, was a long-time leader of the

Seaconke Native American tribe of the Wampanoag nation. He passed away in 2016.

With Jerry's boxing career derailed, he plunged into another brutal blood sport.

Politics.

Working on the Docks of Narragansett Bay

After a round of catching up with friends at various clubs following his discharge, Jerry got a job driving street sweepers at night for the city of Providence.

"It wasn't hard to get a job with the city back in the day. You paid union dues, and that was it."

Jerry was on the 11p.m. to 7am. After his shift, he would go to the union hall at Plain and Public Streets and travel by bus along with other city workers to the docks to unload cargo at Quonset.

The main docks in Rhode Island, better known as The Port of Providence, dated back to 1636 when two small rivers converged into Narragansett Bay and became an active trading post and fishing center. Ships anchored off India Point bringing cargo. Slaves, along with rum, molasses, and tea were unloaded for wealthy merchants like John Brown and others who made fortunes that exist today. Much of Brown University is a testament to the amount of wealth Brown accumulated. Ships from around the world still arrive with automobiles, cement, asphalt, and petroleum.

Jerry worked on the docks from 7 a.m. to 4 p.m. He'd be home around 5 p.m., take a shower, and either go to bed or go out to the clubs.

One of those clubs was The Bronx Tap.

"That's where I met everybody like Ronnie Sweet, Richie Gomes, and the Ouimette brothers, Gerard and John, along with Freddie Bishop and the Green brothers. Everybody was there."

Alfred "Freddie" Bishop, one of the most violent men ever to darken the streets of Providence, is serving life without patrol for a murder he committed in 2009 while on parole for a previous killing. He had served 33 years in prison for a murder committed in 1973. The Superior Court judge who sentenced him to life without parole in 2009 said no one would be safe if Bishop were let out of jail.

Bishop was a frequent flyer at The Bronx Tap.

Gerard Ouimette, another of the most notorious gangsters in Rhode Island, owned the place by strong-arming the original owners. It was a place Gerard could meet with his crew, control who came in, and operate his various bookmaking, loan sharking, and protection rackets.

The police characterized Ouimette as one of Patriarca's most loyal, and dangerous, associates.

Jerry was friendly with the Green brothers although he was considered a person of interest when they were both shot and killed. Police charged Jerry with conspiracy for allegedly procuring the guns used by Ronnie Sweet to shoot Michael Green. Gerard Ouimette's brother Fred received a life sentence for being in the car when the shooting took place.

Richie "Red Bird" Gomes, another Bronx Tap regular, was a violent mobster who died of natural causes in his North Providence apartment in December 2006. He had been a friend of John Gotti and did time for murder. A former State Police captain said, "If there were a New England wise guy hall of fame, he'd be a shoo-in."

Gomes would have a special connection to Jerry. He is

Jerry's first son, Gerry Jr.'s godfather.

Jerry remembered those times and how he could drink, party and get along with them.

"All of a sudden it was total chaos. I don't remember one week out of a year when somebody wasn't fighting with somebody. I wasn't gonna take no shit from anybody, not with my Marine Corps training."

Jerry admitted he had a massive chip on his shoulder after discharge from the Marines. "They fucked me, and that was it."

Between his new friends at The Bronx Tap and a change in the political air in the city of Providence, Jerry found himself lured into dual factions of organized crime. One run by Raymond L.S. Patriarca and the other, the Machiavellian administration of Vincent A. "Buddy" Cianci, Jr.

"I got involved with Larry McGarry, (a long time Providence political operative and Providence Public Works Director under Mayor Joseph A. Doorley, Jr.,) who got fed up with Doorley and wanted to run his own man in a Democratic primary against him. The Democrats ran Francis "Fran" Brown, but Doorley won."

Enter Assistant Attorney General Vincent A. "Buddy" Cianci Jr., a Republican, who announced he would run against Doorley. Cianci had tried three times to put Jerry Tillinghast away but each time didn't get a conviction or had the case dismissed for lack of evidence.

It took some doing, but they talked Jerry and his friend, Al, into working for Democrats for Cianci. Together, they rang doorbells and talked up Cianci, who, despite Doorley's 10 years as mayor, was a decided underdog. They wanted 2,000 votes, Jerry said, and when the results were in on election day, Cianci won by 709 votes.

There were four Environmental Inspector jobs available in

the city of Providence. Cianci knew Jerry and Al were stumping for votes for him and had promised them jobs if he won.

"He gave us the jobs but fired me three times. One time was when I led a protest march against the prison and took a vacation day. I got it back. One time I was sick, and nobody got the message. He fired me again."

The third and final time was when Cianci told him to get him two quarts of oil which he refused to do.

"I said, are you on fucking drugs? Get it yourself."

Jerry avoided termination because his friend, Joe Virgilio, appointed him an assistant shop steward in Local 1033 of the Municipal Workers Union. His union officer status protected him and thus could not be fired.

Of Cianci, Jerry said, "I didn't like him, but I respected him. I think he got fucked by the FBI. (See Operation Plunder Dome.)[3]

---

[3] Plunder Dome was an undercover operation by the FBI started in 1999. The case led to the indictment, conviction, and imprisonment of Cianci.

United States Court of Appeals, First Circuit.

UNITED STATES of America, Appellee, v. Vincent A. CIANCI, Jr., Frank E. Corrente, and Richard E. Autiello, Defendants, Appellants.

Cianci first took office on January 7, 1975, and held it until April 25, 1984, when he was forced to resign after pleading Nolo Contendere to charges he kidnapped and beat a Bristol builder named Raymond DeLeo. Cianci thought DeLeo was having an affair with Buddy's estranged wife, Sheila.

Both DeLeo and Sheila denied the relationship.

After his resignation, Cianci became a popular radio talk show host at a Providence radio station. He often appeared as a guest on the Don Imus radio show. Imus called him the 'thug mayor.' Cianci held his own with Imus in the one-liner department, never giving an inch.

He bided his time by keeping his name in the public eye, then running for mayor in 1990. Again, it was a close race against two other candidates. Cianci won by a small margin. He was so successful this time around, he ran for re-election unopposed.

Then, it hit the fan.

In April 2001, the Department of Justice indicted Cianci, along with several city officials in his administration, on federal charges of racketeering, extortion, mail fraud and witness tampering. It became known as Operation Plunder Dome. This time the jury found him guilty on one of the twenty-seven charges; racketeering. It landed him in prison for five years.

In 2007, he continued his radio career, adding a stint on television, doing political commentary. Diagnosed with colon cancer in January 2015, Cianci died on January 28, 2016. He was 74

Nos. 02-2158, 02-2159, 02-2165, 02-2166, 02-2288.

years old.

Buddy, always one for the best one-liners, quipped at the unveiling of his official portrait in Providence City Hall, "It's not the first time I've been framed."

There is only one Buddy. His one name appellation, which almost everyone in Rhode Island would recognize, was just a bit less well-known than another infamous Rhode Islander who would steer Jerry down a darker path than politics.

Raymond.

As in Raymond L.S. Patriarca. He became the father figure Jerry always wanted through the intercession of Gerard 'The Frenchman' Ouimette.

Another choice, another road. This one would prove a dead end.

Chapter 6 *Fateful Choices*

Window on the Future

Once he settled into life in Providence, his brushes with the law began. During the late 60s and early 70s police charged him with a string of felonies. His first murder charge, for killing Mousie Rotondo, came in 1968. The case was later dismissed.

In February 1969, he pleaded guilty to Assault with a Deadly Weapon.

"I got into a fight with a guy we found out was a federal informant. I came home from work, and this guy had been giving my girlfriend a hard time. He had been looking for someone and swearing at her. I came up behind him, knocked him out, and then threw him down the front steps. He had friends in his car waiting for him. A fight ensued, and he got stabbed a couple of times with an ice pick. I got two years suspended. I drove to Florida to be with my girlfriend, Terry."

The trip to Florida violated his suspended sentence and probation. He returned to Rhode Island and had another encounter with the police.

On April 29, 1970, a young man named Scott Prescott told police that Jerry robbed him at gunpoint and stole $75. Prescott said he was sitting in a Volkswagen bus on Weybosset Street when

Jerry leaned into the vehicle and stuck a gun to his head.

According to Prescott, Jerry told him he could have the money back if he brought him five ounces of marijuana. Prescott was to meet Jerry at the corner of Elmwood Avenue and Burnett Street at 9 p.m.

Prescott and the owner of the Volkswagen bus, Harold Brooks, drove to the police station where Prescott told his story to the cops. He accompanied four police officers to the meeting place at 9 p.m., and the cops arrested Jerry who was unarmed except for a pair of scissors.

The arrest was terrible news for Jerry because of his Nolo Contendere plea to a charge of assault with a dangerous weapon.

In court, Prescott told a Superior Court judge he made up the story about Tillinghast robbing him. The judge refused to believe him and revoked Tillinghast's probation ordering him to begin his two-year prison sentence.

The little jaunt to Florida, which the Judge used to violate the suspended sentence, cost him two years in prison. Jerry appealed to no avail and did the two years.

Jerry said, "I dropped the appeal. The cops would have tortured my family otherwise."

Jerry would marry the girlfriend he followed to Florida, one of his three marriages. First to Jeanne in 1965, for nine days before shipping out for Vietnam, Terry, whom he married in 1969 and who is the mother of his children, and Gloria in 1992 in Florida.

His prison time put him into his first contact with made members of Raymond L.S. Patriarca's organization. Raymond, as he was known throughout the area, was the head of the New England mob and respected by the five major New York Crime families.

Several years later, Jerry was at the ACI on another case when Patriarca returned from the Federal Penitentiary in Atlanta to finish his sentence for conspiracy in the murders of Rudy Marfeo and Anthony Melei. Hitmen gunned down the two men on April 7, 1968, in a grocery store in Providence. Raymond was initially convicted of conspiracy in the murder of Rudy's brother, Willie Marfeo. Willie was killed on July 13, 1966, in a phone booth at the Korner Kitchen Restaurant on Federal Hill.

Police theorized Patriarca ordered the killings.

Patriarca was serving a six-year sentence for Willie and received an additional 10 years for the 1968 murders of Rudy Marfeo and Anthony Melei.

The Marfeo brothers were bookies who had disrespected Patriarca. Melei was Rudy's close friend and bodyguard.

Ironically, it later came out that the star witness against Patriarca, John 'Red' Kelly, lied during his testimony. Kelly and others were implicated in the disastrous FBI involvement with James 'Whitey' Bulger's Winter Hill Gang and FBI agents John Connolly and H. Paul Rico. [4]

---

[4] Kelley testified against Patriarca family boss Raymond Patriarca in a murder case, after which he went into the Federal Witness Protection Program.[6] Kelley gave testimony linking Patriarca and other family members to the murder of Rudolph "Rudy" Marfeo and Anthony Melei. Kelley had been contracted by Patriarca associate Maurice Lerner to kill Marfeo and

Jerry, assigned a work detail as a porter to keep his designated area clean, took the opportunity to meet Patriarca.

Another choice, another path.

"The first time we had a break I walked over to him and introduced myself. He knew of me through Gerard. I told him if there was anything he needed like newspapers or things of that nature I'd get it for him."

Melei, whom Kelley allegedly murdered with a shotgun. [7]

Patriarca and his associates were convicted of conspiracy to commit murder while Lerner also was convicted of murder; the mob boss was sentenced to 10 years in prison. Lerner and the other defendants were subsequently exonerated when it was established that Kelley had perjured himself at the trial, as had FBI Special Agent H. Paul Rico, who had corroborated Kelley's testimony. [8]

Kelley died 10 February 2000 of natural causes in the federal witness protection program

Jerry remembers Patriarca as a man with a lot of personal pride who carried himself well.

"If he didn't know the inmates, he wouldn't talk to them anyway. We all kept the shit heads away. They wanted to go look at him and did that a lot out in the yard."

Jerry came to respect Patriarca, and he earned the man's trust in return. The legend surrounding the man lives on to this day.

Patriarca returned to the ACI from the Atlanta Federal Prison in April 1973 and granted parole on January 9, 1975. He returned to his headquarters at the Coin-O-Matic National Cigarette Service, a vending machine business on Atwells Avenue in the Federal Hill area of Providence.

Jerry was visiting Patriarca later in that office when the old man gave him a hug.

"I can't describe how that felt," he remembered. "It was like a high. I wish he could have been my father, and I loved my father."

These first few stints in prison added to Jerry's reputation as a tough guy after he followed the advice from his older brothers. If he ever ended up in jail, and anyone messed with him, he should make an example so no one else would bother him. Such an incident happened shortly after he arrived in prison.

"There was this six-foot three-inch muscle-bound black guy lifting weights. He was warming up by pressing 250 to 275-pound plates, and I asked him if I could borrow the plates and then give them back to him. He says, 'when I'm done you can have them. Get the fuck outta here'. He pushed up the 275 pounds, and I picked up a 25-pound plate and bounced it off his forehead."

The 275 pounds came down on the guy and nearly broke his neck. Then Jerry hit him again with the 25-pounder.

"How do you like me now? Can I borrow them now?"

The guards came running and made what Jerry thought was a big deal out of it, slapping handcuffs on him and bringing him upstairs. Others in the gym, including Jerry's brothers John and Harold saw the ambulance coming and asked him what happened.

"It's your fault," he told them. "You guys told me if I ever got in a situation, I had to make an example. Well, look at your example."

The monster weightlifter was gone for a couple of months and when he returned came face to face with Jerry. He said he didn't want any problems.

Point made, and that was the end of the issue.

Jerry finished his sentence and returned to the street. It wasn't long before his friends from The Bronx Tap would involve him in more contact with the police.

Christy and the Knockout Punch

It didn't take long for people in and around Providence to realize Jerry Tillinghast was a person to be feared. By the middle 1960s, the country was bracing for racial trouble and Jerry dove right into the middle.

During the 1960s, Providence was little different from other cities rife with racial problems. It had amazed Jerry that race rioting could erupt in Watts, California and make its way to Rhode Island.

But it did.

Trouble in Providence began a year earlier, in August 1966. While cities burned in other parts of the nation, Providence got into the conflict in its own way. Hundreds of people, mostly black, gathered at the Willard Avenue Shopping Center in South Providence. They threw rocks and bottles. Fighting broke out. It was tame compared to Detroit, Watts, and other cities. But still a dangerous situation. State and local police did their best to control the crowd.

Riots were nothing new to Rhode Island's capital city. On October 18, 1824, a white mob attacked black homes in Hard Scrabble in the city's Northwest section after a black man refused to move off the sidewalk when a group of whites approached. The rioting destroyed twenty homes. The damage almost wiped out Hard Scrabble which had sprung up for poor blacks who could live in the inexpensive properties.

Hard Scrabbles were being developed throughout New England in cities in Rhode Island, Massachusetts, and Connecticut. With much of Hard Scrabble gone, another section of Providence replaced the destroyed area. It was known as Snow Town.

During a riot there in 1831, the militia shot and killed four whites. After the incident, voters approved a charter granting strong police powers. It was the birth of police departments in Rhode Island.

Almost a year to the day of the Willard Avenue Shopping Center disturbance, another racially fueled conflict exploded in Providence. This one involved rock and bottle throwing, close to 1,000 police and National Guard personnel, and a declaration by Mayor Joseph A. Doorley, Jr., of a curfew.

The announcement fell on deaf ears.

As the rumbling of trouble began to spread, Gerard Ouimette caught wind of a rumor that blacks were planning on attacking his Bronx Tap.

Militant black leaders had spread the word they wanted no whites in South Providence, prompting Ouimette to meet with them. He received assurances the "keep out" order did not apply to Gerard or his friends.

But Ouimette took precautions anyway, drawing Jerry into

one of his first assignments from him.

During the height of the rioting, mobs attacked whites driving through south Providence. Some had cinder blocks hurled through their windows.

Jerry was home when a family friend named George Ennis stopped by to talk about the trouble. George was known as The Turk and was someone Jerry admired. When the Turk died years later, Jerry was heartsick over it.

The Turk told Jerry of the rumor that blacks would attack The Bronx Tap. He opened the trunk of his car revealing powerful weaponry, including a 30-30 rifle. Jerry grabbed the rifle and a box of shells, walked upstairs, and hid the weapon. When darkness fell, he got a ride to The Bronx Tap bringing the gun with him.

Pulling up to the front, he slid the rifle down the right side of his pants and walked stiff-legged into the bar. Jerry told Ouimette he needed to get onto the roof. The Marine doctrine of tactical positioning kicked in.

With Jerry was another family friend, Jackie Carnavale.

Carnavale asked Jerry if he would shoot the rioters.

"I'm not going to shoot anybody, just fire over their heads."

By now, the crowd was coming toward The Bronx Tap from Blackstone Street. They were carrying chains, an assortment of tools, and other weapons.

Like the Rifleman from the TV show, Jerry blasted away, scattering the crowd which had grown close to 300.

"They started dropping their weapons, enough to open five gas station repair shops. Everyone took off. Jackie Carnavale yelled, 'Oh, my God,' and ran.

"He must have thought he was on the ground floor because he ran right off the roof and landed on a car parked on the street. I thought he was fucking dead."

Jerry climbed down from the roof of The Bronx Tap, wiped his prints off the rifle, and hid it in an alley next to the bar. No charges were ever filed.

Now close friends with several young men at The Bronx Tap, headquarters of Gerard Ouimette, Jerry's frequent visits to the place linked him to Ouimette in the view of the cops.

Known by many as The Frenchman, Gerard Ouimette was a feared gangster. Years later, Gerard would become the first Rhode Islander sentenced under the federal government's 'three strikes you're out' policy. Three federal convictions resulted in an automatic life sentence without parole. He would die in prison. But between now and then, he and Jerry would build an even bigger reputation.

Ouimette established himself in the mob with his penchant for violence. Suspected over the years in several homicides, he avoided any convictions for the killings.

His influence and productivity grew, making him the de facto second-in-command to Raymond Patriarca. Known to most as 'the Frenchman' and to those 'traditional' made men who envied his position as 'that fucking Frenchman,' Ouimette would play a major role in Jerry's involvement in organized crime.

It would be on Ouimette's orders that Jerry faced his most difficult choice.

Within the first few weeks of Jerry hanging out at The Bronx Tap, Rhode Island State Police staged a raid and arrested everyone, including Jerry.

Tending bar was another recent acquaintance, Dennis Greene, who, along with his twin brother, Michael, would figure later in the Tillinghast story. The twins would both meet violent ends at the business end of a gun and Jerry's name would be bantered about as a person of interest.

During the raid, Dennis mouthed off to a trooper who smashed him in the mouth.

One trooper, Bill Tocco, who later became chief of police in the neighboring town of Johnston, tried to steer Jerry away from the place and that crowd.

Jerry, a new face in the crowd, caught Tocco's eye because he had no record yet. Tocco told him to stay away from The Bronx Tap. He added that he would bring him in every time he found his hanging out there.

Jerry had a comeback for Tocco, "Well, I guess we're going to get to know each other quite well. If I want to hang there, I'm going to hang there."

After getting no cooperation, the troopers released everyone picked up at The Bronx Tap. Police didn't find what, or who, they were looking for.

Jerry's status with the Rhode Island State Police would soon change from a new face wannabe in a dangerous crowd to a full-on bad guy.

"Up to then, they had the opinion that I was just a follower, a hanger-on. Later they found out I wasn't a fucking idiot and had my own mind, that I was my own man. Then they started paying more attention."

During these early years, Jerry didn't know the meaning of fear. "One guy or six guys, I'd get in the middle of it and start banging. I didn't give a fuck."

Each of these incidents added to his growing reputation and brought him to the attention of both the cops and people like Gerard Ouimette.

One evening when Jerry and his wife Terry were out for a drive, he became annoyed at a carload of guys following too close. Jerry stopped his car, got out, and told them to back off, receiving the usual response of "fuck you."

"I dove right into the car and started fighting. We got out of the car. I'm doing pretty good. Then, I got punched in the nose. It started bleeding. That really pissed me the fuck off because I didn't know who hit me. But Terry did."

The fight over, Jerry and Terry drove around the area looking for the guy who punched him in the nose. After an hour, they spotted him.

"I punched the shit out of him."

Jerry frequented the Guys and Dolls nightclub on Killingly Street. It was here he had his first encounter with a wise guy by the name of Jerry Christy.

The story added to his growing reputation.

Jerry was enjoying a drink during one of his nightly visits when he noticed a man eyeing him. Minutes later, Jerry walked to the men's room. Several men followed him. The man looking at Jerry thought he was someone else because he threw a punch at him. Before Jerry could retaliate, a friend called Moonie, Richard 'Moon' Diorio, an associate of another noted crime figure, Frank Bobo Marrapese, stepped in and told Jerry to forget it. He was getting into something he shouldn't.

Diorio would come to play a significant part in Bobo's future, testifying against him in a murder case. But at the moment, he and Jerry were still on the way up in the life, and he was doing Jerry a favor.

Angry about the incident, Jerry left the Guys and Dolls and headed for the Peter Pan Diner, not far away, for breakfast.

Just after Jerry arrived at Peter Pan, Jerry Christy pulled up and got out of his car. As Jerry approached the vehicle, Christy turned around and said to him "Oh, there you are. I should knock you the fuck out."

59

"I told him he wasn't knocking me out. We got closer. He tried to kick me. I told him not to kick me, or I'd knock him the fuck out."

Christy tried to kick Jerry again. This time he succeeded.

"I let it hit me, then I hit him with a short left and a straight right and knocked him out." Jerry's educated left taught Christy a painful lesson.

Again, a friend of Jerry's stepped in to stop things before they got out of hand. His name was Arthur Pina. Jerry had gone to school with his brothers at Roger Williams Junior High School.

"We always fought at the school, blacks against whites. Pina and I got to be friends after we left school. So, Pina gets in between us because I told him I was going to fuck Christy up. I said to Pina, what the fuck are you doing?"

By then a crowd of about fifty people had gathered at the front of the Diner. Pina had Jerry's back. That was it for action that day, but the following day Jerry learned Christy and five others were looking for him.

Jerry had a female friend who was part of the Christy crowd. She told Jerry they would all be at Guys and Dolls that night.

Jerry went there and entered through another door where he spotted two of his brother's friends, Albert and Anthony Evans. When the Evans boys realized what was happening their reaction was to pull out guns and say, "let's go shoot them right now."

That wasn't in Jerry's plan. Going up to Christy, Jerry tapped him on the shoulder and said he heard they were looking for him, offering to fight him and the others in his group one at a time.

Christy's lesson at the end of Jerry's straight left from the other night had stuck. He wanted no part of taking Jerry on one to one. He and Jerry shook hands, forgetting the whole thing. Although Jerry didn't trust him. The Evans brother said Christy was a treacherous motherfucker.

Later, Jerry's female friend told him she couldn't believe what he did. She said no one in the state would have done what he did without guns and a bunch of people.

For Jerry, it was his way. Nobody would intimidate him.

Cunningham and the Flying Body

Jerry's antics didn't always involve the police or organized crime members. Some involved dispensing street justice on those who bothered Jerry's friends.

Jerry and a close friend named Larry Cunningham love to tell the story of the guy Jerry threw out a window.

The phone rang at Larry's house at 1:30 one morning. It was Larry's mother, Angela. She was in tears. She and her husband Frank had been living in an apartment house at the corner of Chapin Avenue and Ellery Street in the city's south end, waiting for their new condo to be built.

A party was going full blast in the first-floor apartment. Angela knocked on the door and asked them to tone it down due to the late hour and that her husband was ill. Calling her names, the thugs threatened to throw her out a window and chased her back upstairs.

Larry told his mother to sit with his father on their lawn chairs and away from the noisy party until he got there. Grabbing his gun for which he had a permit, Larry sped toward the apartment from his home in North Smithfield, 15 miles to the north.

Knowing Jerry Tillinghast had an apartment next to them, Angela knocked on his door, but he wasn't home.

Jerry came home just before Larry arrived, and found the elder Cunningham couple sitting in the hallway.

"I could hear the noise and asked Mr. and Mrs. Cunningham why they were sitting in the hallway at that hour," Jerry remembered.

Angela told him a guy in the other apartment said he would throw her out a window. The words incensed Jerry. This was a lovely old couple, no one should ever say that to someone like her.

Jerry told them to go back to their apartment and that he would take care of things.

"I had to bang on the door because the music was so loud. A guy opened the door and said, who are you? I said I live on the second floor. There's an elderly man who is not well, and his wife asked you to turn down the music. Are you the one who said you'd throw her out the window?"

The look on the guy's face told Jerry all he needed to know. He punched the guy in the mouth and knocked him out. Chaos broke out in the apartment.

"I picked him up by the ass of his pants and hummed him through the fuckin' window. I knocked three of them out. I could handle myself. Everybody started bailing out, some through the window where I threw the guy, others piling out the door. I was so fuckin' mad after, I threw everything in the apartment out the window, record player, TV, anything I got my hands on. I piled it all on top of him. Every time I threw more out I'd yell, why not try and throw ME out the fuckin' window you piece of shit?"

No one in the apartment called the cops because they were all high on drugs.

"If I had known, I would have robbed them."

Meanwhile, Larry pulled up just in time to see a human body come crashing through the window of the first-floor apartment, followed by panicked people and furniture.

Jerry recalls, "I think when they said they were going to

62

throw her out the window, that stuck in my mind. So, I threw him through the fuckin' window. I'm glad they didn't say they were going to shoot her because I probably would have gotten my gun and shot them."

After everyone was safe and sound, Jerry went up to his apartment, had coffee and went to bed. He had to get up early for work and stopped to see the damage.

"There was a girl there who said she rented the apartment along with the guy I tossed through the window. She told me she was the guy's girlfriend, but that 'window boy' wasn't coming back. Well, I said, I might have done you a favor."

In between administering street justice, protecting his friends, and working for the city. Jerry and Harold ventured into various business endeavors. One of these was an opportunity to help turn around a failing restaurant in Providence. While the venture would not last long, it added a new dimension to those taking an interest in the brother's activities.

But before that could happen, Jerry had to deal with a 'friendly fire' incident far from the battlefields of war.

A Bullet in the Knee

Jerry did not avoid catching a bullet himself. Considering all the incidents involving guns Jerry may have been involved with, it's remarkable he was only shot once.

The incident can only be called bizarre.

He took a bullet in his knee from a .25 caliber pistol he had given wife Terry for protection.

"I'd been at a bar all night playing cards and lost $180. Then I won back $80 but still lost $100 and got shot on top of that."

When he arrived home early that morning, Terry wanted to

know if he was taking her out that day.

"I said no I am not. I got things to do, and I'm not taking you out. Terry thought I was with another woman. I gave her a small handgun, a.25 automatic. You never know in these neighborhoods. I figured it would be protection for her if she needed it.

"I thought that this ain't right. She's too calm. I used to keep the gun under the refrigerator because of the kids. So, I lifted up the fridge. It wasn't there. I asked her where the.25 was, and she says she didn't know. What do you mean you don't know? The kids didn't move it. She again says, are you taking me out?"

"So I said, 'for the last fuckin' time, I'm not taking you out.' She pulls the gun out of her back pocket and shoots me in the knee. Then she tried to shoot me between the legs but missed. I grabbed it off her and put it in a housecoat hanging on the bedpost. I'm hopping around, pissed. She runs out of the house. A cop sees her running, so she tells him she just shot her husband. The cop asked her who her husband was, and she said he's Jerry Tillinghast.

"That got them all excited.

"I made it to the bedroom to lie down, in walks the police officer. I'm on the phone trying to find my brother Harold to take me to a friend's restaurant. I was going to say some black guy drove by and started shooting and one of the bullets hit me. I never got that far because the cop comes walking through the parlor and into the bedroom. I said, what the fuck are you doing here? I scared the shit out of him. Your wife said you were dead. I said do I look fucking' dead to you? Get outta my house."

It did not take long for other police officers to arrive at Jerry's house.

"By now, I'm on the front porch. One of the cops said, 'what happened to you?' I told him a thousand mosquitoes attacked me.

64

A friend of mine had used it, and I thought it was funny, so I used it."

A superior officer ordered the cop to search the house for the weapon.

"The cop said the house was locked. Well, he said, get the keys. I can't they're in his pocket. I ain't going in his pocket, I'm all alone.

"I said, you put your hand in my pocket and they'll be more blood than what's coming out of my knee. The cops ended up searching the whole fuckin' house and didn't look in the pocket of the housecoat. The found a tiny piece of cocaine and charged me with it. Why the fuck are you charging me with it? I don't live here. Everything was in her name."

A couple of days later Jerry wound up in jail anyway after the cops spotted him on crutches and would have to take him in.

"Take ME in? What the fuck are you taking me in for? They said alimony. I said, are you that fuckin' desperate?"

When Jerry was in jail, friends came to see him and wanted to know the real story.

"They didn't believe me when I said my wife shot me. So, I said, okay. I was driving, and a couple of cars tried to flank me. They pulled a gun and started shooting through the back window, but I got away. They told me that now I was telling the truth. I said you're fucking nuts I'm telling you what happened."

At Rhode Island Hospital Jerry told the doctor he was under too much stress and to keep the cops out of his room.

"The doctor cut the back of my leg, so the bullet was almost falling out. It was like a bulge. I could have taken a pocket knife and removed it. I took the bullet. The cops never asked for it. They charged me with the cocaine, but it was dismissed."

Recovered from the domestic gunplay, Jerry and Terry

agreed on a ceasefire. But as an insurance policy, Jerry disarmed his wife. Life continued on, and Jerry ventured into new endeavors.

Club Martinique

Harold Tillinghast had a dream. It was to have his own restaurant where he could create meals and know the kitchen belonged to him. That opportunity came when Dr. Gold, the owner of The Martinique, a club at 840 Broad Street in Providence, found himself in dire financial straits. Facing the possibility of losing the restaurant, Gold went to a friend, Attorney Paul Dimaio. He asked for help and advice on what to do. DiMaio said he knew someone who could turn things around for him. Paul spoke to Jerry and Jerry went to Harold who leaped at the chance to manage his own place.

Jerry and Harold agreed to bail out Dr. Gold, a local dentist turned businessman, but they had stipulations. The brothers knew The Martinique because they worked there as teenagers. Older brother John worked as a cook there, Harold also worked in the kitchen, and 16-year-old Jerry was a salad boy.

"Immediately, I saw the problem," Jerry remembered.

"It was all white employees in a black neighborhood. I told Harold I didn't want to run the place but would handle security and take care of the hiring and firing. He could run the day to day operation. I wanted $300 a week."

Dr. Gold agreed to let the Tillinghast brothers run the club but would keep ownership. He also gave Jerry money to buy a dance floor and speaker system and turn it into a disco.

"I went to New York, got some ideas and advice, came back and fired all but two pretty white waitresses."

Jerry left the front part of The Martinique open for the bar and closed the restaurant. Where the dining and kitchen areas he made room for pool tables.

"I went to some friends of mine, black guys I knew could handle themselves and use their judgment as to who we wanted to have working with them. I told them if anything happens it's on their heads."

Although the business showed a profit, one issue posed a problem.

Drugs.

Neither Jerry nor Harold could speak Spanish, but they knew the drug problem was with them. They hired a woman to tend bar who spoke Spanish but didn't let on to any customers.

While Jerry sat in a booth reading a newspaper, the woman would give him a signal if anyone was dealing or talking about drugs. One day, two men sat at the bar speaking Spanish and discussing cocaine deals.

Jerry approached the pair and asked them if they spoke English.

The dealers shook their heads no.

"I told them I knew they spoke it and told them not to do drugs in here."

He warned them, in no uncertain terms, that they could not deal drugs in, around, or anywhere near the club.

"I said the last thing we needed was to have the police pull a raid and find drugs. If they did, these guys were going to pay the price."

'How much?' they asked, misunderstanding what Jerry was saying.

"I said no, I don't want a piece of the business. I don't want it here at all. If I catch you dealing, or if the cops come here looking for you guys because you're dealing, I'll break your fucking neck and legs. Don't disrespect me."

Jerry told his bouncer to keep an eye on the pair, but they got the message. There were no problems with drugs

Within two and a half months, Dr. Gold found himself in the financial black. Harold wanted to buy The Martinique, but it was never to be. The brothers were arrested and charged with murdering loan shark George Basmajian.

Former Providence city councilman Nicholas Easton, now an Assistant Professor in the Department of Political Science and Public Administration at Columbus State University in Georgia, developed an interest in public service early when he lived in one of the poorest neighborhoods in Providence.

In 1976, before becoming a member of the city council where he served for 12 years, Easton was a young leader in the Progress for all Inclusive Care for the Elderly, known as PACE. He and other members of the group got wind of a plot to torch The Martinique.

"Arson fires around the 4th of July were a big problem in the city. We created a neighborhood patrol to cut down on the number of fires," he said. "We had a tip that Dr. Gold wasn't doing well as the owner of The Martinique and that the Tillinghasts were going to have it burned to get the insurance."

Easton went to Tom Doyle, the Fire Marshal, and told him the Tillinghast were about to bum The Martinique for the insurance money. Doyle said he would put a 24 hour a day watch on the club and station firefighter's cars around the building.

That 4th of July passed without incident at The Martinique. But with Jerry and Harold out of the picture, the business continued to decline.

By 1979, it was closed, and the Tillinghast brothers had begun long prison terms. The Martinique, with no one to run it, lay abandoned and decaying.

It eventually burned down. Police thought Jerry and Harold had some involvement, perhaps hoping an insurance claim would fund their appeal. But a later investigation indicated an explosion blew out a wall. Doyle's investigators found the probable cause was a gas leak and no one was ever charged.

Doyle would later change careers and become a waiter at another Rhode Island institution in Cranston, Twin Oaks restaurant. Often some of Jerry's former associates in the mob would be seen at the bar and enjoying the renowned food.

In Rhode Island, there is only one degree of separation.

Chapter 7 *Charges, Trials, and Dismissals*

By 1968, Jerry was fully integrated into The Bronx Tap crowd, and Gerard Ouimette took more interest in him. Jerry's fearlessness and toughness might prove valuable if he could be trusted.

That remained to be seen, but it didn't take long for Jerry to prove his mettle.

Harold, older and better known in the neighborhood at the time, was like Jerry in many ways but lacked the anger and pent-up rage.

While Harold could hold his own, he avoided physical confrontations unless they were absolutely necessary. His criminal record reflected his aversion to violence.

Jerry, on the other hand, never walked away from a fight. He ran at them full force. One guy or six, if they provoked Jerry, he was coming at them.

While Harold and Jerry differed in their propensity toward violence, Harold was still getting deeper into the world of bookmaking and other mob activities.

Harold's less violent tendencies could be perceived as a weakness. They were not. He was just less willing to resort to it unless it was unavoidable.

The differences between the two men became evident one night in the fall of 1968.

Mousie Trap

Early in the chilly, drizzly morning of November 12, 1968, Jerry sat in the Peter Pan Diner waiting on his brother, Harold. He walked outside to look for him, finding Harold hiding in the shadows holding a pump-action shotgun. From the look on Harold's face, Jerry could tell he was in over his head.

Jerry took the shotgun and sent his brother back inside.

A car pulled up.

"Where's Harold?" the driver asked.

"He's not here, you got me," Jerry answered, and jumped in the car. It was one of those choices, Jerry would say years later, that he wished he could take back.

The car drove off into the night, and Jerry went down an uncertain path. It would lead to his first serious brush with the law.

News stories and police investigative reports tell the parallel story of what followed Jerry's fateful choice.

Anthony Rotondo was a 34-year-old small-time hoodlum, nicknamed Mousie. At 3:45 a.m. on that same November 12, 1968, he was sleeping on a table at the Forum Club in the Federal Hill section of Providence, Rhode Island.

The little man made his living running dice games without permission of Raymond L.S. Patriarca. An unwise and dangerous choice.

Mousie had several arrests for assault and robbery over the

years but served only a few months in prison when he was 19 years old.

He was a hustler and con artist, but hardly intimidating.

Mousie's luck ran out that morning. He probably never felt the shotgun blasts fired from inches away that put 200 pellets into the right side of his head.

Someone had left the door to the Forum Club unlocked. Police theorized that was how the two men they would soon arrest gained entrance.

Nearby, just before 5am, police spotted a car with two men. They chased after them, finally locating the vehicle in front of a house at 169 Almy Street.

Neither man resisted arrest. They were identified as Ronald Sweet, 33 and Jerry Tillinghast, 23.

Jerry threw the car keys away before the cop pulled up behind them. He asked why they were being questioned, claiming they were just sitting in the car.

The cop told Jerry he had received a call about a shooting in the area. They were looking for suspicious people, and they fit the bill. The officer asked for Jerry's I.D. and license and went back to the cruiser to check it out.

A backup arrived.

They told Jerry and Ronnie to get out of the car and put their hands on the roof. The cops handcuffed them and placed them in a police van. The cop who initially stopped them asked his fellow officers why they were being arrested. They said a shotgun shell had been discovered in the back seat.

Whatever the case, the cops had them in custody.

"When he pulled us over the cop said he saw something thrown out of the car. He was fucking lying about the shotgun and shell. He just wanted to impress his fellow officers. We were in the wrong place at the wrong time."

One officer scouted the area and found the keys Jerry had tossed. He opened the trunk and got quite a surprise.

"They almost shit their pants. They said 'what are we gonna do with all this shit? What they found was two license plates from out of town, one from Florida and one from Ohio, a pair of Playtex gloves and a 12-gauge pump shotgun."

A different version of the story has the cops finding the shotgun inside the house, hidden in a toilet tank. The police never found a shotgun shell.

As with most stories involving Jerry, what happened depends on who is telling the story.

Both were charged with murder and questioned for the next 72 hours. Jerry remembered growing tired of the questioning and told police he would finally talk, in a manner of speaking.

"They got out a typewriter and asked me where I had been. I told the cop I was fucking your mother."

As Jerry reached for a phone to make his allotted call, one of the officers broke his hand with a blackjack. Other officers had to cover their mouths to keep from laughing.

Both Ronald and Jerry were taken downstairs for further questioning, but police got nowhere. According to Jerry, they beat Ronnie until the bruises on his body matched the purple shirt he was wearing.

They were held for 90 days. The shotgun seized when they were arrested was sent to the FBI Crime Lab in Washington, D.C., but nothing came of it.

With little cooperation and no witnesses or evidence to tie the two to the murder, the police realized there wasn't enough to go forward with a trial.

Reluctantly, the cops had no choice but to release them.

Jerry's explanation was more straightforward. "There was no evidence because we didn't do it."

It was a scenario that would play over and over. A murder, an arrest, and insufficient evidence to prove anything. During the late 60s and early 70s, Jerry would face a total of five murder charges and one conspiracy to commit murder.

Most were dismissed for lack of evidence.

Except for the last one. That one would stick. But there were more choices to make before then.

After the Rotondo case against Jerry and Ronnie Sweet fell apart, Jerry's star began to rise in Gerard's eyes. He brought Jerry into the fold, relying on him for more and more tasks.

In these early years of Jerry's involvement with Gerard, he'd be witness to the shifting loyalties among the men who operated in this world.

Loyalty had a short shelf-life when it came to money and power. A friendly drink one night often ended with gunfire and dead bodies.

The police took notice of this growing association between Ouimette and Jerry. They soon added him to the 'usual suspects' list whenever a hit went down, or a big score happened.

Ronnie Sweet, Jerry's co-defendant in the Mousie Rotondo homicide, found himself charged in another murder along with Gerard's brother Fred Ouimette.

The case would be another in a string of incidents where the police tried, without little success, to tie Jerry into the operation of Gerard's violent campaign to control his turf.

October 1969: Michael Green Murder

On October 21, 1969, Michael Greene was gunned down on

the street outside his home on Althea St., in Providence. After the shooting, Providence police arrested and charged Ronald Sweet and Fred Ouimette for the murder.

On Jun 19, 1970, a jury found Ouimette and Sweet guilty of murdering Michael Greene. Both received life sentences. Jerry Tillinghast almost went with them.

In an appeal of their conviction, the Rhode Island Supreme Court detailed the circumstances of the shooting.

"This is an indictment charging that on October 21, 1969, Frederick J. Ouimette and Ronald H. Sweet, Jr., hereinafter referred to as Ouimette and Sweet, murdered one Michael Greene, hereinafter referred to as Greene. The defendants were tried before a justice of the Superior Court sitting with a jury during June 1970. The jury returned a verdict of guilty in the case of each defendant. Subsequently, a motion for a new trial filed by each defendant was denied, and each defendant was sentenced to imprisonment for life. Each is now prosecuting a bill of exceptions in this court.

It is not disputed that Greene was shot to death at about 8 o'clock on the evening of October 21, 1969, while standing between two cars parked parallel to one another on Althea Street in the city of Providence. The evidence discloses that Greene and Donna M. St. Rock, hereinafter referred to as St. Rock, were friendly and often went out together. On that evening St. Rock and her cousin, Christine Choiniere, hereinafter referred to as Choiniere, had driven Greene from his home on Althea Street in Providence to a gas station located on Broadway in that city. Choiniere was driving the car, St. Rock was riding next to her in the front seat, and Greene was riding beside St. Rock. At the gas station, according to the testimony of Choiniere, Greene had gotten out of her car to talk for a couple of minutes to the occupants of a dark blue car that had come into the gas station immediately after they had driven in.

After Greene returned to Choiniere's car, they left the gas station to return to Althea Street. While driving along Althea Street, Choiniere realized that the car she had seen at the gas station was following them. Apparently at the suggestion of Greene, she parked her car on the right-hand side of Althea Street at the curb. The car following then came alongside of Choiniere's car and parked about two or three feet to the left of her car. Greene alighted from Choiniere's car and, leaning on the door of the other car, began talking to the occupants while she and her cousin, St. Rock, remained in her car. According to her testimony, she suddenly heard several shots, felt glass from the windshield striking her in the face, and, upon alighting from her car, found Greene lying on his back in the street. His body was parallel to her car, and his feet about opposite the door of the driver's station.

According to the further testimony of Choiniere, she had had an opportunity to see the face of the passenger in the other car when it pulled alongside. After a few moments she was able to observe the driver's face. Thereafter, she identified Ouimette as the driver and Sweet as the passenger in the car that parked alongside hers. She had identified the two defendants, first, from photographs in the possession of the police and, secondly, during the course of two separate lineups at the state prison.[5]"

They charged Jerry with conspiracy in Greene's shooting for allegedly helping to procure weapons used in the murder. Gerard Ouimette and his brother John were also charged in the plot. The case was based almost exclusively on the testimony of William H. Miller, Jr.

---

[5] https://law.justia.com/cases/rhode-island/supreme-court/1972/298-a-2d-124-0.html

The whole thing began at the ACI after an incident between Perkins and Gerard's brother, John. Gerard Ouimette wanted revenge for Perkins beating John.

Miller, a fellow inmate at the ACI who had made friends with Gerard, told police Gerard offered him $5,000 to kill Perkins. Greene was added to the plot since he took part in the beating of John Ouimette.

Miller was paroled on September 30, 1969. Instead of taking up Gerard's offer, Miller cooperated with the police after witnessing the shooting.

The details of the conspiracy are spelled out in Gerard Ouimette's appeal of his conviction.

"The conspiracy trial was held before a Superior Court jury in early 1972. The trial lasted 8 weeks. The prosecution's chief witness was William H. Miller, Jr. Miller testified that he had met petitioner (Gerard Ouimette) while they were both incarcerated at the Adult Correctional Institutions. He claimed that they worked together in the prison laundry and that as a result of this association a friendship between the two ripened to such a point that Miller, at petitioner's urging, agreed to kill a Homer Perkins for a price of $5,000. Later, the agreement was broadened to include as a second victim one Michael Greene who had allegedly beaten up petitioner's brother, John. Miller was paroled on September 30, 1969. Once he was on the street, he contacted John Ouimette, and they along with a Ronald H. Sweet, Jr. and a Gerald M. Tillinghast embarked upon a plan whose ultimate goal was the elimination of Perkins and Greene. Miller detailed a series of meetings with his fellow conspirators, the procurement of firearms, and the periodic reconnoitering of the different places where Perkins and Greene were likely to be in each other's company. Miller testified that on the evening of October 21, 1969, while he was walking along the street upon which Greene lived, he saw Greene

leave his car and approach another car. Shots were fired, and Greene was killed.

A number of witnesses testified for the defense. Each witness contradicted some aspect of Miller's testimony. Two depositions of prisoners who served time with Miller when he was at a federal penitentiary in Leavenworth, Kansas, were read to the jurors. The thrust of their contents was that Miller had told the affiants that he knew nothing about Greene's killing but that in view of the other charges then pending against him and because of police persuasion, he would appear as a prosecution witness against petitioner and hope that his cooperation would cause the Rhode Island authorities to show a similar cooperative attitude toward him.

The jury returned guilty verdicts against petitioner and Sweet and acquitted petitioner's brother John and Tillinghast. The petitioner and Sweet filed a motion for a new trial and in support thereof they filed as newly discovered evidence an affidavit signed by Miller's wife. In her affidavit, the wife asserted that her husband had lied at trial; that Miller remained at home the night of Greene's death; that contrary to her husband's courtroom testimony, Miller had never remained away from their home without her at night within the period during which he was allegedly planning the demise of Greene and Perkins; and that she had advised two Providence police detectives of "these facts." The detectives filed counter affidavits in which they denied ever having any conversation with Mrs. Miller about her husband's association with petitioner, his brother John, Sweet, or Tillinghast.[6]"

Miller testified he had been walking near Greene's home. He

---

[6] https://law.justia.com/cases/rhode-island/supreme-court/1975/342-a-2d-250.htm

saw a car follow Greene's from a nearby gas station and pull up behind him. Greene got out of his car and walked to the second vehicle. Suddenly, shots rang out, and Greene fell dead.

Police arrested the occupants of the first vehicle, Fred Ouimette, Gerard's younger brother, and Ronnie Sweet who was the shooter. At the murder trial, both were found guilty and given life. Gerard was found guilty of conspiracy, but Jerry and John Ouimette were acquitted.

Jerry's record of beating cases continued.

In a bizarre twist that remains mysterious to this day, Sweet told the appellate court that Fred had nothing to do with the murder and had no idea why he was following Greene. Neither did he realize Sweet had a gun. The court didn't buy the story, and both spent a long time in prison.

Homer Perkins committed suicide by shooting himself the night before he was to begin serving a prison sentence for another crime. Jerry maintains Perkins was so scared that he couldn't face being in the same area as Gerard.

Once again on the street after winning in court, Jerry's reputation as a force to be reckoned with, and a difficult target to convict, rose.

In between this acquittal and late 1974, Jerry had some minor brushes with the law. One of those violated his probation conditions putting him back behind bars for two years.

Those two years would prove instrumental in raising Jerry's profile both inside organized crime and with the cops investigating the mob.

An opportunity to meet and talk with Raymond L.S. Patriarca, facilitated by fortune and a good word by Gerard, brought Jerry to the old man's attention.

Among Patriarca's abilities was recognizing those who could

be useful to his organization. He saw something in Jerry, and this was all it took.

Jerry's star was on the rise with the approval of the old man. He did his time, returned to Gerard's fold, and his productivity and success within the crew increased.

While Gerard and Jerry were prohibited by heritage from being 'made' men, they had the horsepower many made men never achieved.

The full story of the next major incident involving Jerry took years before it bubbled up to the police. A cooperating suspect, using his inside knowledge to reduce his own prison time, would unveil the story as part of another significant case.

The police suspected Gerard of the mob hit on Joseph Schiavone from the beginning and, by association, so was Jerry. But presuming who committed the crime is a long way from arresting them for it.

Schiavone Homicide November 1974

November 27, 1974 was a bright, seasonal day in Cranston, Rhode Island. Sometime around 3:30-3:45 p.m. Joseph Schiavone backed his 1966 Buick into his driveway at 99 Coldbrook Drive.

Several men approached the vehicle and opened fire. Schiavone died in the hail of bullets and blasts from a shotgun.

The sound of the gunfire shattered the ordinarily sedate residential neighborhood. The phone lines lit up at the Cranston Police station.

Officers found Schiavone in his car, dead from the gunshot wounds, the top of his blown off and his brain matter scattered through the interior.

The gunmen were long gone. On the ground, the police located three shotgun shells.

The investigation focused on identifying the body and locating any witnesses. Once the police had a name, they knew it was a mob hit. People would be reluctant to talk. Memories would disappear. Willful ignorance became the rule of the day.

Except for two young men who, upon learning what happened, reported a strange encounter they had with several men near the scene of the homicide.

One of the young men told the police of seeing three men in the parking lot carrying what looked like a pipe. He said hi to the men, but they didn't answer him. At the time he could only give a vague description of the men.

A second young man reported seeing a blue van pass by him as he stood at the end of his driveway waiting for a ride. He saw the van turn from Coldbrook Drive onto Coldbrook Court, which is a dead-end with a turnabout circle. The witness described the driver as a white male approximately 35 to 38 years of age, dark hair, Italian descent, with a mustache. He said the man had a wrinkled face and shabby appearance.[7]

He watched the van loop around the circle, drive up the street, and turn left onto Coldbrook Drive toward the Schiavone house. He then walked to his backyard and stood on a wall that gave him a view of Merit Drive to watch for his ride. After a few moments, he heard five gunshots, then saw the same van turn down Merit Drive.

Other witnesses corroborated the route taken by the van.

---

[7] State Police Internal investigative reports of Lt. Anthony Mancuso

Police later recovered a stolen van they believed involved in the hit. Abandoned inside, they found a ski mask with several strands of human hair, a sawed-off 12-gauge shotgun, and a.38 caliber Colt Agent revolver.

Schiavone, a bookmaker and loan shark, had a history with violence and the law of the street. Two of his long-time associates, brothers Willie and Rudolph Marfeo, were gunned down for not paying Raymond Patriarca a portion of their bookmaking and loan shark business.

Schiavone was suspected, by both the cops and Gerard Ouimette, of trying to orchestrate a hit on Gerard. Ouimette believed Schiavone sent a guy named Joe Pine to take him out.

Ouimette arranged a 'sit down' with Schiavone to settle the matter. Schiavone denied orchestrating the hit. For a time, the truce held.

But the only thing stable in the world these guys operate in is instability.

Schiavone continued to run an independent operation without the proper payoffs to Raymond through Gerard. That is inexcusable in the mob monopoly controlled by Patriarca.

And there were rumors.

Rumors of Schiavone talking to the police. If failing to pay up is a sin, talking about the business to the cops was a capital offense.

Failing to pay gets you a beating, talking gets you silenced. Permanently.

Once Schiavone proved more of a liability than an asset, he had to go.

The cops suspected Gerard of arranging the murder but charging him would take evidence. With no other witnesses, lots of suspicions, and no firm suspects as the shooters, the case lay dormant.

Another in the long line of Rhode Island mob hits languishing for lack of evidence.

Until Robert Joseph Dussault, in custody for the Bonded Vault Robbery, began cooperating with the police. He told Sgt. Anthony Mancuso of the Rhode Island State Police an intriguing story.

But that was yet to come. A bribe to a prison guard sets in motion a prison break and a reunion of partners in crime, Robert 'Deuce' Dussault and Charles 'Chucky' Flynn. Ultimately leading to Dussault becoming a key government witness and breaking open several unsolved crimes.

Chapter 8 *Patriarca, Ouimette, & Gotti: Misplaced Loyalty*

John Gotti: Teflon Don

It was inevitable that Jerry Tillinghast would someday meet John Gotti. He met him with Gerard Ouimette on his frequent trips to New York.

"He was a very charismatic guy. I found him to be pretty intelligent. When I met him, he was a captain in the Gambino crime family and a protege of Aniello Dellacroce, the Underboss."

When Jerry met him, Gotti was a rising force in the New York mob. He had plans, big plans, to take over the organization and run things his way.

Aniello Dellacroce was his mentor. Dellacroce himself had once been considered in line to take over the family, but it was not to be. Dellacroce accepted the decision and stayed Underboss, Gotti had no intention of letting someone else determine his fate.

A criminal indictment set in motion events culminating with Gotti fulfilling his ambition.

The FBI indicted Gotti and his crew for selling drugs. Acquitted after this and a series of other trials, the press gave him the name 'Teflon Don.'

But Gotti feared he was marked for death by the Gambino people who wanted no involvement in the drug business. He decided to take fate into his own hands.

As part of his move to take over, Gotti orchestrated the murder of Paul 'Big Paul' Castellano, head of the family. He was gunned down outside a favorite restaurant in December 1985. Later trial testimony said Gotti watched the hit from across the street, unable to remove himself as other, more experienced, bosses might have done.

Gotti's move paid off. He would ascend to the head one of the most influential crime families in the country. All this would come years later.

"In '76, '77, and early '78, I'd be up in New York all the time with Gerard. It was always friendly visits. We talked mostly about sports."

Other topics would come up that didn't concern him, so he kept his mouth shut. "It was none of my business. If they wanted me to know something they would have told me."

During one trip to New York, without Gerard, Jerry saw some of Gotti's guys but didn't stop in to see John. When he got back to Providence, Gerard asked where'd been.

"I told him, New York, why?"

"John said if you ever come to New York again without stopping to see him, he'll put up roadblocks so you can't leave. I liked John. He was personable and funny. He wanted me to stay on in New York for a while and work with his crew, but I knew what that meant. I'd be the outside talent nobody knew. I didn't need that. I had my own thing in Providence, and that was enough for me."

Jerry recalled how much Gotti loved his family. "That was another thing I respected about him."

In March 1988, Gotti's 12-year-old son, Frank, was riding his mini-bike on the road when a neighbor, John Favara, struck and killed the boy. The death was ruled an accident, but Favara soon disappeared. One rumor was that Favara was cut in two with a chainsaw. Police believe Favara, an employee of Castro Convertible and a backyard neighbor of Gotti, was shot to death and his body put in a barrel of acid to dissolve it. No trace was ever found, and no one ever charged.

Gotti's method of managing his people taught Jerry something about loyalty, or the lack thereof. One thing Jerry learned listening to Gotti and other's talk, loyalty had a short shelf-life in their world.

"Listen to them, that's what I would do. Say nothing, just listen. John and Gerard would discuss things; business, people, whatever. One minute they'd be smiling and offering a guy drinks, next minute, as soon as the guy walked away, they'd be calling him an asshole lowlife. I often wondered what they said about us when we weren't there.

"Look, sometimes they'd let me hear, sometimes not. Didn't matter, if they wanted me to know something they'd tell me. Otherwise, I mind my own fucking business."

Jerry pauses a moment." I'll tell you one thing, and I said it to Gerard on the way back one time, listening to Gotti, and the others talk about other crews, and their own fucking crew for that matter, I came to realize they were a bunch of treacherous motherfuckers. I told Gerard, after listening to them we're lucky we're French and Irish and not Italian."

Raymond L.S. Patriarca

To explain the fascination with organized crime in Rhode

Island, one has to come to know the man who wrote the story, Raymond L. S. Patriarca.

Patriarca was born in Worcester, Massachusetts on March 18, 1908. His family moved to Providence, settling in Federal Hill.

Within a few years, Patriarca was arrested for hijacking, armed robbery, safecracking, and auto theft. It was prime training for involvement with the rising Italian Mafia.

Patriarca's reputation grew in the 1930s, 1940s, and 1950s as he rose in the organization. The Providence Board of Public Safety designated him as Public Enemy No. 1 when he was in his mid-twenties.

In Massachusetts, he was sentenced to five years in prison for robbery. But he was paroled in 1938 after serving just a few months.

An inquiry revealed that Executive Councilor Daniel H. Coakley, a close associate of Governor Charles F. Hurley, had drawn up a parole petition based on the appeals of a Father Fagin whom Coakley had fabricated. Coakley was impeached and dismissed from the Governor's office. This scandal enhanced Patriarca's reputation in the underworld, as it demonstrated the power of his political connections[8].

This wouldn't be the last time a priest became involved in a case involving Patriarca. At a later trial, a priest would testify as an alibi witness for Patriarca. His testimony would later fall apart. The priest said it was an innocent error, the evidence would prove otherwise.

In the 1950s, Phillip Bruccola, then the head of organized crime in New England based in Boston, fled the country to avoid prison on tax evasion. Patriarca moved to fill the void, eventually

---

[8] https://en.wikipedia.org/wiki/Raymond_L._S._Patriarca

relocating the base of operations to Providence.

Operating out of a small vending machine company, Coin-O-Matic on Atwells Ave, Patriarca consolidated his power with brutality and unmitigated violence.

By the 1960s, the Justice Department, headed by Robert F. Kennedy, set its eyes on organized crime. Patriarca was subpoenaed to testify before the Senate, and his appearance was seen on evening newscasts around the country.

Unintimidated by Kennedy or anyone else, Patriarca was belligerent, argumentative, and gave no ground in his claims of persecution due to his Italian heritage.

Kennedy, determined to topple Patriarca's growing influence and control over organized crime not just in Providence but nationally, ordered the FBI to bug the offices at Coin-O-Matic.

For almost three years, the FBI listened and recorded conversations with the inner sanctum of the Patriarca's world.

When President Kennedy was assassinated, Lyndon Johnson became President. He did not approve of using electronic surveillance on American citizens, regardless of the purpose, and ordered the bugs removed.

Although the FBI hadn't obtained a court order authorizing the bugs, rendering the recordings inadmissible in court, it didn't prevent tidbits from leaking out.

Not all were of a sinister nature. On amusing recording came after Patriarca had received the subpoena to testify before Congress. A young, former Cumberland Police Officer turned U.S. Marshal, John Partington, delivered the summons. Patriarca called his attorney and complained he had just been served by a 'boy scout.'

Partington would go on to set up and run the Witness Protection Program. Many of the witnesses who would testify against the mob were protected by Partington and the marshal's service.

Just another Rhode Island connection to the connected world of organized crime.

The reach of the mob knew no limits in myth and reality. Rumors of mob involvement in the Kennedy assassination and CIA plots to kill Fidel Castro added to the Patriarca legend. His name having been linked to a contract on Castro through his associate Maurice 'Pro' Lerner.[9]

All throughout this era, Patriarca could be seen sitting in front of his business, smoking his cigarette.

To anyone unfamiliar with the man, he had a grandfatherly appearance of a shopkeeper. To those more intimately familiar with the name, he was to be feared, admired, or avoided depending on one's point of view.

In March 1970, Patriarca and several of his associates went on trial for murder and conspiracy. John "Red" Kelley, armored car robber and mob hitman, who afterward went into the federal witness protection program, was the chief witness.

Kelley gave testimony linking Patriarca and other family members to the murder of Rudolph Marfeo and Anthon Melei. Kelley testified Patriarca gave him the contract to kill Marfeo.

Patriarca and his associates were convicted of conspiracy to commit murder; associate Maurice Lerner was convicted of the actual murder. The mob boss was sentenced to 10 years in prison, but he continued to run his family while imprisoned.

Lerner and the other defendants were subsequently exonerated when it was established that Kelley had perjured himself at the trial, as had FBI agent H. Paul Rico, who corroborated

---

9 https://www.nytimes.com/2016/10/30/sports/baseball/maurice-lerner-prospect-turned-mob-hitman.html

Kelley's testimony.[10]

Patriarca's integration into the fabric of Rhode Island life is underscored by a little known, but startling, comparison of Patriarca with another Rhode Island legend.

When Colonel Walter Stone, a former Providence police officer during the early years of Patriarca's rise but best known as the longest-serving Superintendent of the Rhode Island State Police, passed away his former Executive Officer, Major Lionel Benjamin, compared the respect the troopers had for Stone to the respect Patriarca's men had for him.

It was a telling, if troubling, analogy. But it was with this reputation that Patriarca entered Jerry's life.

Jerry was serving a two-year sentence at the ACI when he first encountered Raymond L.S. Patriarca. Returning to Rhode Island pending his parole in the conspiracy to commit murder charge, Patriarca was placed in the same cellblock area as Jerry.

Jerry held the job of porter, keeping the area clean and him out of his cell much of the time. It was an opportunity for Jerry to meet the man who was a living legend in Rhode Island.

"I waited for a while for Mr. P to settle in and get his cell straightened out and then went over and introduced myself and to ask him if he needed or wanted anything. He said he didn't, and I mentioned to him if he did need or want anything that I, or one of the other porters, would get it for him and that we would check with him daily. He stayed in his cell reading or resting a lot."

Jerry remembered watching the other prisoners reacting to Patriarca especially during nice weather when he tried to catch some sun.

"That was a hard thing for him to do because as soon as he

[10] Partington, John (2010). *The Mob and Me: Wiseguys and the Witness Protection Program*. New York: Gallery Books. pp. 123–4. ISBN 978-1-4391-6769-4.

went out in the yard and sat at a picnic table, the other guys would sit with him and start talking about business and sports or anything just to be talking to or with him. As for myself, I used to just stand in the background and watch and study who was who and try to figure out who was really who," Jerry laughed.

"This went on for a while, during the day or the evening, until it started to get cooler out. Then he would go back inside to his cell to retire for the night. I think he went inside just to get away from all that nonsense they used to bring up to him just to have something to say so they could probably tell people that they were talking to him just to impress someone."

It was on a weekend morning that Jerry connected personally with Raymond L.S. Patriarca.

"One Saturday morning for some reason he didn't feel like going out. I went to see if he wanted anything or if he was feeling sick, but he just said he didn't feel like going out and I thought he was just tired of listening to those nitwits with their petty bullshit. There were at least five or six people he would talk to privately before he would even listen to the rabble each day. So, I had the morning paper with me and gave it to him and started to walk away and he said for me to stay for a few minutes. He wanted to ask me something. I said okay, but I didn't do it. I was laughing when I said it, and he was laughing too."

What transpired between the two would change Jerry's life.

"I asked him if there was something he wanted me to do for him and he said yes. I said, okay you name it, and you got it, and I was still smiling. He asked, could I answer one question. He took me totally by surprise when he asked me why I don't ask questions or talk when everybody else does. I wasn't sure how to answer as I said, Mr. P., I don't understand the question.

"He said I go outside every time everyone else does and

always stand off to the side and never say anything or ask any questions. Now, I'm getting a little nervous and thought I was doing something or did something wrong. He saw how I was nervous, and he told me to relax that it was just a question. So, I did what he said and tried to relax, and then he repeated it, that all accusing word, why?

I waited a few seconds and told him. I said I didn't ask anything or want to know anything that didn't pertain to me. I felt that if you wanted me to know something you would tell me and until you did that whatever anyone, especially you, was talking about was none of my business, and I didn't need to know it. If I offended you, I am very sorry. He said he didn't want me to be sorry but that he wanted me to do something for him. Of course, I said yes."

Patriarca wanted Jerry to go out to the yard the next day and tell the hangers on the same thing he told him. Patriarca told Jerry maybe then he would go out and have a little peace. Then, they both laughed.

Jerry said, "He would always talk to me like a father, and that's how I came to know him and respect and love him. I feel that he was a great man and still is in my eyes. I am truly grateful for having met and known him and for the way he touched my life. Thank you, Mr. P. To try and sum it up a little better when Mr. P passed away, so did Rhode Island. May you rest in peace my friend and father figure. I miss you very very much."

Jerry did earn loyalty from a few people. A group who remain loyal to this day

True Friends and Loyalty

Jerry's many friends have remained loyal to him despite his frequent brushes with the law. They have also stayed true during extended periods of incarceration, including the 30 years he was behind bars with Harold for the Basmajian murder.

One of those long-time friends is Vinnie DeQuattro who has been Jerry's barber for more than 40 years. He also cut the hair of Raymond L.S. Patriarca, who would call ahead for an appointment, pull up to the shop on Broadway, and quickly enter. Raymond didn't like to wait for a second. He'd get his hair cut and then leave as abruptly as he arrived.

George Basmajian was one of Vinnie's customers. Vinnie says George was always trying to screw him out of money. Most of the men thought to be connected to the underworld, especially around Broadway and Federal Hill came in.

Born in Italy 70 years ago, Vinnie has been cutting hair for nearly 50 years. On the wall of Vinny D's Barber Salon hangs a picture of himself with a neatly dressed and newly cut Jerry. Vinnie had just won a barbering competition in Boston held in 1976 and to clinch victory he had to cut Jerry's hair in front of a group of judges.

Police had spotted the photo of the two of them and told Vinnie to remove it. Vinnie did not, and it hangs there today.

"The picture stays until I die," he told police.

Authorities, including at least one FBI agent, have questioned Vinnie about his relationship with Jerry Tillinghast over the years, but it was basically a waste of their time.

"If somebody's loyal to you, you gotta be loyal to them," Vinnie says of his long relationship with Jerry, his brothers, and his children. All of whom had their hair cut by him.

Vincenzo DeQuattro was born in Italy and raised in Caserta where his father urged him to study bricks and mortar and become a mason.

The night before Jerry and Harold were charged with killing George Basmajian, Jerry had his haircut by Vinnie.

"I went home to bed. The next morning I'm listening to the radio and hear Jerry's name about the crime. I figured I lost two customers, Jerry and George," he laughed.

In Jerry's world, one often lived by the sword and died by the sword. An older man Jerry thought a lot of was 67-year-old Louis 'The Fox' Taglianetti who was gunned down one night outside his apartment complex in Cranston. It was February 1, 1970. Taglianetti was with his much younger girlfriend, who was also shot to death.

"I liked him very much. But shooting his girlfriend wasn't right. You just don't do that."

Jerry met Taglianetti in 1968 when he was incarcerated at the ACI during the investigation of the Mousie Rotondo murder in the nightclub on Knight Street.

"We hit it off immediately. I thought Louie was a great guy."

Taglianetti was responsible for the murder of Jackie "Mad dog" Nazarian. It was Nazarian who helped arrange the 1957 hit on the head of Murder Incorporated, Albert Anastasia, as he sat in a barber's chair at the Park Sheraton Hotel in New York City.

Several names cropped up as Anastasia's killer including Joe "Crazy Joe" Gallo from the Profaci crime family and a drug dealer from the Gambino crime family with Rhode Island ties, John "Jackie" Nazarian. It was a crime never solved. Anastasia had been one of the most ruthless criminals and feared members of Cosa Nostra.

Nazarian bragged that he would be a better crime boss than Patriarca. He never got the chance to prove it. Nazarian was shot five times leaving a dice game on Federal Hill in 1962.

Taglianetti's end came when the FBI released tapes it had on

94

him during his trial for income tax evasion. When the feds turned those tapes over to prosecutors, some of the same material included wiretaps on Patriarca's Atwells Avenue headquarters. Those recordings severely damaged Patriarca's control over the New England Mafia.

So, who killed The Fox? Rumors pointed to another long-time crime figure, said to be the second most powerful figure in Rhode Island behind Patriarca, Dickie Callei.

The 41-year-old Callei met his own ugly demise in March 1975. His body was buried in a shallow five-foot deep grave in the town of Rehoboth, Massachusetts, just over the Rhode Island line. He had been stabbed in the face, chest, and stomach, shot five times at close range, and struck on the head several times with a blunt instrument.

Jerry has pat answers for people frequently asking him what he did as an enforcer for the Patriarca Crime family. Whenever someone writes about crime and criminals in the heyday of organized crime in Rhode Island, they refer to Jerry Tillinghast as an enforcer. Conjuring up an image of a man breaking legs, arms, and teeth at the behest of Raymond L.S. Patriarca, the crime boss of New England.

Jerry's answer to the way he's described is simple.

"They can call me anything they like. But never, not one time was I ever convicted of being an enforcer or being involved in organized crime.

"I'm not saying I never did anything. I did thirty years for the one thing they convicted me of. But until that case, they never proved anything in the arena.

"They just didn't like losing in court so tagging me with a name was the best they could do."

Chapter 9 *Bonded Vault August 1975*

The Robbery

The story of the Bonded Vault Robbery is a legend in Rhode Island. Through widespread media coverage and the trial record, it is easy to piece together what happened.

Like most things, the truth lies in the simplest explanation.

This was not a well-orchestrate plan to get rich, the loot was a bonus.

This was not the plan of diabolical criminal geniuses who planned the perfect crime. Some suspect it was always an inside job.

This was not the heist of the century, unexceptional were it not for the value of the loot. Although the actual amount has never been decisively established.

It was retribution. Pure and simple.

Bad guys robbing bad guys because of a perceived slight. A failure of respect valued over and above all else by the catalyst of the crime.

It was a way to send a message and make a profit. Making people pay for their mistakes with their own ill-gotten goods. For some of those who did the grunt work, the messengers with the muscle, it would prove ultimately self-destructive.

It was Instigated by none other than Raymond L.S. Patriarca himself. Planned by his trusted associates the Ouimettes; Gerard 'The Frenchman' and his brother, John.

A secret bank in an unassuming commercial building in a modest area of Providence would soon draw attention from every major law enforcement agency in the state and the FBI.

All because the head of the New England mob was not happy. On his return to Providence after his parole from the ACI in January 1975, Raymond Patriarca took offense at the amount of money raised on his behalf. He chafed at the insufficient show of respect.

To Raymond, respect was everything. Men who violated the rule of respect paid a hefty price, often with their lives. This latest insult would not go unpunished. Those who profited from his leadership and, more troubling to the old man, to his absence would learn the penalty for such disrespect.

Loyalty and respect were not negotiable.

Another of the tidbits to leak out of the illegal bugs in Patriarca's office was this gem.

"In this thing of ours, your love for your mother and father is one thing. Your love for the family is a different kind of love.[11]"

Patriarca, backed by the muscle of Gerard Ouimette's crew, was about to show those who insulted him the meaning of that line.

---

[11] New England Mafia Fades Away - The Boston Globe. (n.d.). Retrieved from https://www.bostonglobe.com/metro/2012/05/07/new-england-mafia-fades-away/dynRDS

And the price for ignoring it.

Police say it was his son, Raymond 'Junior' Patriarca, who told John Ouimette about the score. The information about the secret bank may have been unknown to the general public. But it was no secret to those in the dark world of the mob and their minions. Chucky Flynn and others knew where it was, they also knew better than to move on it.

John Ouimette put the plan together on Gerard's orders. They all knew this only happened with Raymond L.S. Patriarca's consent. No one would be stupid enough to do it on their own.

Ouimette rounded up a crew. The target was the Hudson Cold Storage Company at 101 Cranston Street in Providence. This location housed the well-guarded, but not entirely unknown, secret; the Bonded Vault Company and 150 private safe deposit boxes. Most of them huge.

The operation was an insider-only place to store things needing a not-so-legitimate form of confidentiality; a place to hide stuff you didn't want the cops or the government to know about. Stolen property, cash, and other proceeds of criminal activity, it didn't matter. With the right connections, anyone was welcome.

All with no questions asked.

According to the police and the official court record, the crew met in a ranch house at 5 Golf Avenue in East Providence, rented by one of the crew, Charles "Chucky" Flynn. Chucky was an escapee since he broke away from a work-release program in Massachusetts.

Living with Flynn at the time was Robert Dussault, known as Deuce, also an escapee from a Massachusetts prison. Joining him was Joe "The Dancer" Danese, Lawrence "Mitch" Lanoue, Robert Macaskill, Ralph "Skippy" Byrnes, John Ouimette, brother of Gerard Ouimette who was in prison, and Jerry.

Jerry recalled. "I'd been to the house a few times. I met Chucky (Flynn) a few years earlier. We'd hit it off right away. I knew he'd walked away from a work-release crew at Walpole so whenever I went there, I'd use different cars and take a different route, so no one followed me there."

Of the crew, Byrnes was the odd-man out. No criminal record, just a gambler who wanted to be with the tough guys. His absolute loyalty to Gerard, he was on the crew as Gerard's eyes and ears, would later come to haunt Jerry.

Byrnes' aspirations within Patriarca's organization would drive him to interfere even with Gerard's plans if it suited him. Stories of Gerard's failed efforts to kill Rudolph Sciarra bubbled up. It wasn't luck that saved Sciarra, it was Byrnes tipping off Nicky Bianco to the hit and warning Sciarra ahead of time. But for this score, Byrnes played his part.

After Ouimette explained the job, several drove by 101 Cranston Street. Each had tasks to do. Another Ouimette brother, Walter, handled stealing a van to deliver the crew and haul the loot away.

Dussault was the point man. Unintimidated by anything, he'd be the first in the door. His face uncovered and eye to eye with the victims. He was unconcerned about being identified. He planned to be long gone from Rhode Island before the cops had a chance to locate and arrest him.

The rest were muscle. Strong backs to crack the safe deposit boxes, empty the contents, and load the loot into the van for the getaway.

They took a few days to organize and gather the equipment. Dussault and others practiced the route they would follow back to Golf Ave.

As the tension built, the friction between the men grew.

Dussault considered bailing out but his loyalty to Flynn, something that would save his life if not his lifestyle during a tense encounter after the robbery, compelled him to stay in.

According to police reports, with the plan in place and ready to set in motion, the robbery was delayed a day. Someone, with both knowledge of the job and the influence to control it, needed time to remove items from the location.

Most suspected it was Raymond 'Junior' Patriarca. While it added to the growing frustration, there was not much they could do about it. Like it or not, they waited.

According to discussions among the defendants while they awaited trial, Junior Patriarca wasn't the reason for the delay. Jerry thinks the cops wanted to add to the story by lumping in Patriarca's son every chance they had.

"If he had stuff there, and they took it, it was going to him and the old man anyway. What would be the point? Chucky said the only reason they delayed it was a problem with the van. The day before Walter (Ouimette) was standing near the van and a cop saw him. They dumped the van and stole another in case the cop remembered him."

It was a hot morning on August 14, 1975, when the group of men entered The Hudson Furs Company. They filled duffel bags with cash, gold coin, silver bars, and jewelry; most of the stolen items loot belonging to mobsters. Secrets are only safe if no one knows about them. Patriarca knew all the secrets.

Dussault was first in. Wearing a suit and carrying a briefcase, he approached the door. Hudson Furs was closed for vacation this fateful day. Typically, there would be fifteen employees. Today, as the robbers knew, there would be fewer people inside.

Sam Levine, his two brothers, Hyman and Abraham, Hyman's wife Rosalind, and the company secretary, Barbara Oliva were there catching up on business matters.

The door to the office had a buzzer, Sam Levine looked up at the man and buzzed him in. It begs the question if the business was closed, and Levine didn't know or expect Dussault, why let him in? Jerry says he often wondered if the timing and cooperation were not just luck, but inside information.

This part of the story is reconstructed from the official court record. While Dussault entered the building, the rest waited in the van.

Sam looked at the man, "Can I help you?"

Dussault pulls out a piece of paper, ignoring Sam, and reads softly. Aggravated by the intrusion, Sam walks to the counter to deal with Dussault and send him away. Instead, Sam feels the cold steel of a revolver pushed against his nose.

Dussault warns him not to trigger any alarms or "I'll blow your head off." Sam follows the command. "Who else is here?" Dussault demands.

Sam tells him about the other four. Dussault has him call them out one at a time. Within minutes, Dussault has them all gathered together. During the trial, some macabre comedy moments came out about those first few moments.

Barbara Oliva, who would be the other star witness at the trial, looked at Dussault's gun, just inches from her face, and said, "Are those real bullets in that gun?"

"What are you, a fucking comedian?" Dussault growled.

Oliva, scared but not intimidated, replied, "I've seen guns before. Get that god-damned thing out of my face."

The standoff was interrupted with the first of the crew, Chucky Flynn, entering the building and struggling to pull on a mask. Soon they are all inside and the work to smash open the boxes starts.

Dussault and Flynn hand pillowcases to the employees, forcing them to put them over their heads; all except for Sam. They need him if somebody shows up. Which happens while the work is in progress. Sam's uncle, an elderly gentleman named Max Gellerman, arrives and is quickly added to the group of hostages.

Dussault guards them while the robbers go to work prying open safe deposit boxes and filling seven duffel bags. While the results were spectacular, the process was a chaotic, unorganized, conglomeration of yelling, swearing, jostling, and raw muscle power prying the boxes open. It wasn't a smooth movie-like orchestrated production, it was more a bumbling group of adrenaline-fueled men flailing away, stumbling toward an unimaginable mountain of loot.

Through sheer determination and adrenaline, they emptied 146 boxes. It took between seventy-five and ninety minutes. They had specific ones they were to look for but went after as many as they could with brute force, if not finesse.

Despite the stifling heat, crowded environment, and sweat pouring from them, the size of the haul spurred them on.

Loading the van and a couple of cars, the combined weight of the men and loot causing the back ends of the vehicles to sag as they fled the scene.

In the last act, Dussault herded the employees into a small bathroom and blocked the door. Waving the gun to underscore his point, he warned them to stay inside, or he would shoot them.

They did, for a while, until they feared they would run out of oxygen. With some effort, the employees forced the door open. Before them lay an unimaginable scene.

Knee deep on the floor was cash, jewels, gold, silver, and other valuable items. The robbers left as much on the floor as they hauled away.

Reports have the Levine brothers scooping up much of the stuff left behind and squirreling it away. That would be a risky business if the information from the so-called "Patriarca Papers" is to be believed.

The "Patriarca Papers" was a compilation of over seven thousand pages of FBI reports, arrest files, and intelligence information released under a Freedom of Information Act request by Golocalprov.com reporters. The site published an in-depth analysis with the aid of a team of experts on organized crime.[12]

A significant portion of the file focused on the Bonded Vault and the speculation about who was behind the robbery and where the loot went

According to FBI intelligence reports released with the Patriarca papers, known as '302s', an informant told agents that not only did Patriarca sanction the robbery but that he, in fact, owned the business, although there would be no public records.[13]

If that was the case, any goods 'left' behind might have still ended up with the old man courtesy of the Levine brothers. If not, the Levine's recognized a unique opportunity and seized the moment.

No matter which version was accurate, the score was a big one for whoever got a piece of it. Jerry believes it was always an inside job. He points to several reasons for his thinking.

"One, Johnny (Ouimette) had a list. Who would they get a list of box numbers and names from? Second, there was a buzzer

---

[12] http://www.golocalprov.com/patriarca-papers/
[13] http://www.golocalprov.com/patriarca-papers/fbi-files-the-patriarca-papers-entry-49

on the door. If they were closed for vacation, and someone they didn't recognize or expect was at the door, why buzz him in? No doubt in my mind somebody inside that place was involved."

The FBI informant from the 302-intelligence report supports Jerry's point. Raymond's influence and control of Providence were vast and well-concealed. The inside job makes sense when you consider both independent sources.

The Bonded Vault Robbery, as it became known, would become the stuff of legends. Since those who kept things there did so to hide secrets, no one would be very forthcoming with the police. It would be a perfect crime, for some. For those who did the dirty work, it was less than ideal.

The thieves regrouped at the house in East Providence and divided up the take. The cash totaled $704,000, not counting the small bills; the ones and fives. Five thousand is set aside for Walter Ouimette's stealing the van. The rest is divided among the others. Dussault, Flynn, Byrnes, Danese, Lanoue, Tarzian, Macaskill, John Ouimette, and according to the police, Jerry.

Each received $64,000 in cash with the promise of more to come.

It never did.

Gerard Ouimette and 'Il Padrino' Raymond L. S. Patriarca got the bulk of the precious metals and jewels. It is clear from the information revealed at trial, and the investigation, that the men tried for the case never got any more than the sixty-four thousand dollars in cash.

Gerard and Raymond orchestrated the robbery and, as was often the case, used the men as the muscle; never intending to share the most valuable part of the stolen goods.

Who took the jewelry, coins, and silver away from Golf Ave? Skippy Byrnes and John Ouimette.

When Dussault ultimately cooperated with the cops, he would tell them that Byrnes loaded the jewelry into a suitcase. He described the handle of the case as having band-aids wrapped around it. During the execution of search warrant at Byrnes apartment six months after the robbery, the police recovered a suitcase matching the description. It would be this suitcase that convicted Byrnes at trial.

The case against each of the six defendants hinged on the testimony of two other participants, Robert Dussault and Joe Danese. Their testimony was the only direct evidence tying Jerry and the others to the robbery.

The assumptions of the police based on the involvement of Gerard Ouimette's brother reinforced the information Dussault and Danese offered. They rounded up the usual suspects and moved forward with the case.

But assumptions are not evidence. It would be up to the jury to decide who was guilty or innocent.

Paul Dimaio, who defended Jerry in the Bonded Vault case, argued that Harvey Brower, Byrnes' lawyer, should have filed a motion to suppress the search warrant since the information used to obtain it was stale.

Dimaio, just a young attorney at the time, stood up to the other lawyers in his approach to the case.

"I never asked Jerry what happened. It's not necessary for an effective defense. My job was to ensure the government presented a fair, ethical, and legal case. The alibi witnesses came forward of their own free will. It came down to this, the defendants whose alibis were challenged by the prosecution were convicted. Those whose alibis were not challenged, including Jerry, were found not guilty. In Byrnes case, failing to move to suppress the suitcase was a major error."

There was more to the case strategy, but that comes later.

The estimates of the value of goods stolen have varied over the years. In the book, The Last Good Heist: The Inside Story of the Biggest Single Payday in the Criminal History of the Northeast by Tim White, Wayne Worcester, and Randall Richard, the authors write,

"Unsavory truth needs time, and when federal and organized-crime sources confide their final estimate of the take to three reporters' decades later, the figure is stunning. Not more than one million, or even four million as earlier thought, but upwards, they say, of thirty-two million, and that's in 1975--at least one hundred forty million dollars today.[14] *"*

The actual value is forever buried with the bodies of the men who orchestrated it.

Maybe.

Jerry says the one thing he knows is the guys who did the job got their share of the cash, and nothing more.

" Here is the way I did things," Jerry says, "I got paid for what I did. I didn't expect more because that's the way it is in that world. I had a lot of respect for Gerard, but nothing he did would surprise me. That's the only way to do things in that world."

The crew may have been promised more would come, but it was an empty promise. The jewels, gold coins, and silver went elsewhere.

---

[14] The Last Good Heist: The Inside Story of The Biggest... (n.d.). Retrieved from https://www.goodreads.com/book/show/28646699-the-last-good-heist

Raymond Patriarca and Gerard Ouimette wanted to make a point about respect but only insofar as it was respect for them. The guys they used to pull off the job weren't on the same level. They got what they got, and that was all they should expect.

How does one dispose of such items, particularly in the tiny State of Rhode Island? You don't. Jerry believes the bulk of the goods went to New York, fenced with the assistance of John Gotti and Aniello Dellacroce.

"Gerard could be like that sometime, he'd lie about things. Manipulate people to get them to do things his way or get what he wanted. Besides, it was none of my business. End of story."

"If I had to guess, all the stuff from Bonded Vault went to New York, and they took care of getting rid of it. How much they got, I have no idea. Who knows? Gerard kept a lot of things to himself, and I didn't ask."

It makes sense considering the close association between Patriarca in Providence and Gotti in New York. Money makes people happy and seals the bond of what passes as friendship in that world.

In Gerard's book, *What Price Providence?*[15], he chose three pictures to put on the cover; Raymond Patriarca, John Gotti, and Gerard Ouimette. A closer, more sinister, association would be hard to find.

Whatever happened to the loot, the investigation by State and Local police would ultimately lead to one of the most remarkable trials in the history of Rhode Island. It pitted the best of the Attorney General's office against a dream team of defense

---

[15] https://www.amazon.com/What-Price-Providence-Gerard-Ouimette-ebook/dp/B0084H8BUW

lawyers. Some of them familiar names in mob-related cases. One was a young, less known, but up and coming lawyer named Paul Dimaio, whose career would take off after this case.

But that was yet to come. The work of the Providence police, who did the bulk of the investigation, along with the Rhode Island State Police and the FBI, would lead to the arrest of a cast of characters and a trial for the ages.

The Investigation

Local, State, and Federal Law Enforcement all sought information from a variety of informants and street sources. Sometimes, they shared information. Most often they didn't.

One of the most troubling inefficiencies in law enforcement is the myth of cooperation. Internecine rivalries are a plague on solving cases. This case would force them to cooperate, although the bulk of the work was done by Providence police detectives.

One name bubbled up to each agency, Robert 'Deuce' Dussault. Once they had his name, the rest would fall into place.

Dussault was the easiest to identify since he never wore a mask. Flynn soon followed when Barbara Oliva, despite having the gun pointed at her face, recognized Flynn, whose bumbling with his mask gave her enough of a look to remember him. With these names came the inevitable links to Patriarca's organization and the most likely culprits, Gerard 'the Frenchman' Ouimette's crew.

The cops didn't need anyone to tell them this. The streetwise cops knew nothing of this magnitude happened without Raymond having a hand in it. The list of possible suspects became clear and limited.

A grand jury was convened. Within a month of the heist,

Dussault was indicted on twenty counts including armed robbery and kidnapping. Law enforcement now focused on finding the man everyone knew as Deuce.

They weren't the only ones. Gerard Ouimette had concerns about Dussault. He feared if the cops got to him, Dussault would give them all up. A newspaper article claimed an attorney from Massachusetts was negotiating Dussault' s surrender.

This did not make the Ouimette, or Raymond Patriarca, happy.

After the heist, most of the men tried to lay low and stay off police radar. Dussault, Chucky Flynn, and Chucky's girlfriend Ellen, who would soon become his wife, left for Las Vegas for some gambling and fun.

In Vegas, Dussault met a hooker named Karyne Sponheim. They quickly became an item, moving in together. Living the lifestyle of the rich and infamous, blowing through the money. Dussault returned to his roots, robbing various places to maintain his lifestyle. He also made another error in judgment.

He complained to Chucky about needing more money and the fact they hadn't gotten anything else from Ouimette.

When Chucky and his girlfriend returned to Providence, he too was out of money. Here, there is two versions of what happens next. In one, John Ouimette sends Flynn with Joe Danese and Skippy Byrnes back to Law Vegas with orders to kill Dussault. In Gerard's book, _What Price Providence?_[16] Gerard claims he sent Jerry to Vegas with Flynn, Byrnes, and his brother John.

Jerry says he never went to Vegas, but Byrnes would do

---

[16] https://www.amazon.com/What-Price-

Providence-Gerard-Ouimette-ebook/dp/B0084H8BUW

anything Gerard asked him to do.

That's the thing about these stories, mixed in each version lies the truth. One thing is clear, Flynn and some others went to Las Vegas to kill Dussault.

Chucky and Deuce were old friends. When confronted in Vegas, instead of gunfire there was the memory of their long-standing friendship. They reminisced about old scores and their time together in jail. Flynn decided not to kill his friend. He returned to Providence, telling Ouimette he'd spoken to Dussault and he was not going to rat them out.

Another error in judgment.

Gerard warned them, Dussault would be a big problem if they didn't take care of things. From <u>What Price Providence?</u>

"Johnny came to visit me, bringing me the news that Chucky had let Dussault off the hook. I got sick when I heard that and told Johnny, 'John, you'd better go clean up your act. Whatever loose ends you have, take care of them. Whatever Dussault knows about your business, you'd better dispose of the evidence. You're all gonna get pinched.[17]*"*

While Gerard may not have convinced John of the error of his ways, his prediction of Dussault becoming a problem soon came to pass.

Dussault's temper was about to do them all in.

Deuce frequently beat Karyne. Sick of it, she went to the police and then fled to her mother's home in California. Deuce was left alone in Karyne's apartment. Karyne called the manager to get him removed. The manager called the police.

---

[17] https://www.amazon.com/What-Price-

Providence-Gerard-Ouimette-ebook/dp/B0084H8BUW

The cops showed up and took Dussault into custody. He was carrying two phony identification cards. The police called in the FBI, suspecting they had Dussault. Identifying people back then was not as efficient as it is today. Pictures can be deceiving. For a while, Dussault stuck to his story; the cops had the wrong guy.

It didn't last.

Here again, there is a conflict as to who broke Dussault down with a lie. Some say it was the FBI, some claim it was Tony Mancuso from the Rhode Island State Police. In either case, they told Dussault that because Chucky hadn't killed him, Chucky had been whacked by Joe Danese. Dussault, understandably upset, admitted who he was. With Dussault in custody, and thinking about talking, Mancuso and Providence Detectives Pat Rocchio and Bill Giblin continued the ruse and applied more pressure.

They told Dussault he too would soon be killed. If he wanted protection, he had better start talking. Dussault turned into an Olympian rat. He named everyone involved, including Raymond L.S. Patriarca and Gerard Ouimette as planners. Dussault signed a statement. After they had his statement, Mancuso told Dussault Chucky was still alive and in police custody.

All's fair in love and war. When it came to organized crime, the cops were at war.

Dussault knew he'd been had. Soon after Dussault returned to Rhode Island, the cops convinced another member of the crew to talk.

Joe Danese also began cooperating with the police.

With the story from the two participants, more grand jury indictments followed, and the hunt was on to round everyone up.

The Arrest

Jerry has vivid memories of that day in January 1976. He and six-year-old Gerry Jr. were in the basement of his apartment on Chalkstone Avenue in Providence setting up a pool table. His wife at the time, Terri called downstairs to tell him the police were surrounding the house.

"What house," he asked?

"Our house," she answered.

The next thing he knew, the police rushed in with guns drawn.

Jerry remembered yelling at the cops. "Hey put them fuckin' guns away. I got my family here.' They had guns drawn, and I was holding a pool stick. They yelled I was under arrest, drop the stick. 'Drop the stick? It's brand fucking new. How 'bout I put it down'. I told them again to put the fuckin' guns away and stop scaring my kid.

I put the cue stick down and put my hands out. I'm not stupid, I don't fight with cops. Unless they throw the first punch, but that's on them."

Within minutes, Jerry was in handcuffs and on his way to State Police headquarters. He yelled to Terri to call his lawyer, Paul DiMaio.

Throughout the case, Jerry stuck to his story. "You got the wrong guy. They knew better than to ask me to make a statement," Jerry smiled. "That wasn't ever happening. Told them what I always tell them. See you in the arena. That's what I call going to court, the arena."

Little did he know that this case would be more than an arena, it would be a full-blown Roman Circus.

For eight and a half months Jerry would be held without bail at the state prison. Four of those months would be on trial in a courtroom in Providence played out before a daily packed house filled with armed with Rhode Island State Troopers, Providence cops, FBI agents, and a curious public.

Cocky as ever, Jerry was so sure he would be acquitted of the twenty counts of armed robbery and extortion against him, that he sent his clothes home two weeks before the verdict.

During the trial in Providence Superior Court, Jerry's 16-year-old sister, Sissy, organized a protest over what she and other family members and friends thought was an unfair proceeding, especially when they thought available exculpatory evidence was not being presented on behalf of the defendants.

"There was evidence that wasn't heard. When you went into the courtroom, it was basically like a strip search," according to Sissy.

"The defendants had no rights, so we got together some family and friends. We walked up and down in front of the courthouse. We had a guillotine there with a dog's head in it. It said "Satan has more rights that inmates do. We did that for about five days."

Chapter 10 *Bonded Vault Trial*

The Defendants

On indictment number, P-1-1976-0053, the State of Rhode Island charged the following defendants with robbery, kidnapping, and a host of other criminal offenses.

John Ouimette, Charles 'Chucky' Flynn, Ralph 'Skippy' Byrnes, Jerry Tillinghast, Walter Ouimette, Jacob Tarzian, Lawrence 'Mitch' Lanoue and Robert Macaskill. At the time of the trial, Lanoue and Macaskill were fugitives and not yet in custody,

Two individuals who played a key part in the indictment by agreeing to testify, Joe 'the Dancer' Danese and Robert 'Deuce' Dussault.

Both were granted immunity for the robbery and promised leniency in other matters.

While not listed as defendants, three names were a constant presence during the case; Raymond L.S. Patriarca, Raymond "Junior' Patriarca, and Gerard Ouimette.

The nature of the score, and the reticence of those 'victimized' by the robbery to come forward with claims lent "credibility to the hearsay," as a Judge would later rule.

Everyone assumed there was no way such a score took place without Patriarca's blessing. Most believed it took his specific orders to make it happen. With Gerard's brother, John, and cousin Walter Ouimette charged as participants, it took no leap of faith to know Gerard had a hand in the matter.

These guys were his crew. They did what he told them to do.

As they awaited trial, Flynn and the others talked about what happened.

"Chucky told me they divided up the cash. While counting it, they heard someone outside the house. Everybody pulled out guns thinking it was the cops. Chucky went outside and talked to the guy. They were there to put up storm windows. Chucky came back and told everybody to relax. They all stuffed their money in bags and left in different cars. Johnny (Ouimette) and Skippy (Byrnes) put the jewelry, silver bars, and coins in a suitcase and took them."

The distinctive tape around the handle, as described by Dussault, would lead cops to execute a search warrant at Byrnes' apartment where they found the suitcase.

Law enforcement sources learned that some of the money from fencing the goods, fifty-thousand dollars, went to pay lawyers and fines for Nicky Bianco's tax case. It all makes sense considering the close association between Gotti and Gerard Ouimette. Bianco was part of Gotti's crew so there would be a strong loyalty there.

Another link between Gotti and Providence was Richard "Red Bird" Gomes. Originally from Providence, Red Bird was Gotti's driver during his rise in the Gambino crime family. Gomes' close association with Patriarca--he eventually moved back to Providence--and his being trusted enough by Gotti to be his driver is just another dot connecting Providence to New York and the most logical way they disposed of the loot.

In his book, Ouimette writes,

_"The late 1970s and early 1980s were good...I was traveling a lot to New York to see my friend, John Gotti. Things were going well *for him and we would go out to dinner by ourselves frequently. Whenever I'd go with him to a wake or a wedding party, he would introduce me to a skipper in another crew. John would say, "This is a captain in so and so's crew. I'm gonna introduce you, give Raymond Jr. a boost." John was always thinking ahead. Raymond Jr. should've noticed the kind of good men he had around him. But it took going to prison to open his eyes. There he learned about real men and how few and far between they were and how lucky he was to have such good friends, guys like Bobo Marrapese, my brother John, Ronnie Sweet, Jerry Tillinghast, Skippy, Matty Guglielmetti, and me. We would go to the grave before we would hurt anybody by ratting on them.[18]"*

That loyalty Gerard bragged about later ended when he went to prison and wrote the book. His association with Gotti being one of the few stories corroborated by other sources. But this was all down the line, Jerry had to get through the Bonded Vault trial first.

He learned quite a bit listening to Chucky Flynn.

"While we were awaiting trial, Chucky told me about going to Las Vegas with Skippy and Joe the Dancer to find Dussault. In his book, Gerard said it was me who went with them. He could be like that sometimes, say things that weren't true to complicate an issue or make himself sound more in control.

"I never went to Vegas, never been there. That was on them, nothing to do with me. Chucky and I were close, I liked the

---

[18] What Price Providence? By Gerard

Ouimette. Page 237

https://www.amazon.com/dp/B0084H8BUW

guy. Did his job, kept his mouth shut. He could've buried all those guys, but he just stood up and took it."

Some of the defendants on trial may have gotten a big payday from the score, but only the most naive among them believed they'd ever see anything else. Those greedy enough to ask about it became targets and, when they learned of the double cross, turned to the cops for protection in exchange for their testimony.

As is always the case, greed gave birth to the idea and greed brought down some of those involved.

The Prosecutors

The Department of Attorney General, Providence Police, Rhode Island State Police, and the FBI built a strong case against the defendants. But it would be up to a jury of average Rhode Islanders to decide if it was enough to convince them of the crew's guilt.

It would all come down to trial.

Leading the case for the state was Albert DeRobbio. It would be his last trial as a prosecutor before he became a Judge, eventually rising to be the Chief Justice of the Rhode Island District Court.

DeRobbio was smart, tough, and acerbic with little tolerance for either the mob or their stain on his Italian heritage. Something he shared with the trial judge, Anthony Giannini. They both took the mob's influence and control in Rhode Island as a personal insult.

Easy to anger, the defendants would take advantage of DeRobbio's quick temper during the trial. Whispering to him under their breath, laughing at things he said, or otherwise trying to interrupt his game plan. He often took the bait, adding to the circus-like atmosphere.

Assisting DeRobbio was John Austin Murphy. Admitted to the bar just 2 years earlier after graduating from Boston College School of Law, it quickly became apparent why Murphy was chosen. His knowledge of the law, analytical mind, and ability to identify strengths and weaknesses in witnesses made him invaluable to the case.

Aiding the prosecutors was Detective Sergeant William "Billy" Giblin. There were many good street cops in Providence. Cops that knew the lay of the land and the people who lived there, both good and bad. Giblin was one of the best. He understood the mob mentality better than most. Better than some of the men who lived it. The cops were fortunate he was on their side, a couple of different life decisions and Giblin would have been a formidable opponent.

It wasn't as congenial a team effort as one would hope. There was a subtle but evident hostility between the Providence cops and the State Police. The FBI was viewed by both as poaching on their turf. Each agency vying for primacy in these high-profile cases.

At one time, Giblin had the Rhode Island State Police emblem hanging over his desk where he would joke about, "the mighty state police are always watching." His personal pronouncement of his misgivings about working with them.

One might wonder why agencies tasked with the same purpose would resist cooperation. It was the rule of shit rolling downhill. Providence saw the State Police show up for the big stuff but nowhere to be seen for the day to day gritty reality of urban police work. The State Police experienced the same with the FBI with agents swarming with resources whenever headline cases broke.

This inter-agency rivalry could sometimes be overridden when cops, troopers, and agents developed relationships over cases. But the history between the two primary agencies, Providence and the State Police, in the 1960-1970s was still one of intense disdain. Some of that was due to the policies of Colonel Walter Stone. The Superintendent of the State Police and a former Providence cop, Stone feared the corrupting influence of daily street contact with the mob and associates. Keeping his troopers on a tight rein to avoid the close interaction on the street typical to local cops.

Some of it was simple mistrust bred from rumor and innuendo. Over time, it would change. But for this case, the atmosphere roiled with distrust between the cops and the troopers.

Somehow, DeRobbio and Murphy managed to focus the inter-agency rivalry on the real goal; convicting the men who robbed Bonded Vault and putting them in prison for life.

The Defense Lawyers

In a criminal case, at least in theory, the defense has no obligation to prove anything. All the defense must do is establish reasonable doubt in the mind of one juror, and their client walks.

Most defense attorneys focus on more than just reasonable doubt. They go after the credibility and motivations of witnesses, question evidence and how it was handled, and offer alternative theories on the case. Piling on doubt. No matter how irrational these explanations may be, the defense knows it need sway just one juror.

The state must convince all twelve.

In this case, the defense attorneys were seasoned, experienced, and, with some of the lawyers, determined to win regardless of the ethical lines they might cross. The Patriarca shadow could often darken the most moral of attorneys.

The defense team was a who's who of top legal criminal lawyers. John 'Jack' Cicilline, Patriarca's long-time legal adviser and confidante, Harvey Brower, another long-time mob attorney later disbarred from practice, Harris Berson, Salvatore Romano, Jr., later convicted of conspiracy in a mob-sanctioned break-in and disbarred, and Paul Dimaio.

During the bail hearings, a lawyer from the law offices of Edward Bennet Williams, one of the most famous criminal trial attorneys in the country, participated in the case. It shows the reach of the Patriarca organization.

Paul Dimaio recalled a discussion with the lawyer from William's office.

"At the end of the bail hearing when everybody was held without bail, that lawyer from Williams' office (his name escapes me) told me that they were not going to go any further because this case was not winnable. I told him that's nice, but I was a native here, and I had no choice but to follow through with a case that I thought needed to be defended, winnable or not and try to win."

In later cases, William Kunstler, another famous civil rights attorney, represented the Ouimette crew. The reach of the Patriarca organization, and the depth of their resources to afford such representation, was extensive.

As the trial drew close, the maneuvering, legal and otherwise, began.

Notes would be left for the prosecutors with addresses of family and friends. A dozen dead black roses were sent to the hotel where the jury was sequestered; the implied message designed to intimidate.

Both sides claimed it was the other's efforts to influence the jury.

These guys didn't play fair, but DiMaio wasn't part of it. He focused on defending his client as his most important responsibility.

The other defendants' approach to their defense was simple, let Chucky Flynn's lawyer be the only one to file for discovery.

It was a simple, if disingenuous, plan. It was also a complete surprise to the DiMaio and the court.

While each defendant is entitled to their own defense, some of the attorneys insisted on a single defense strategy. Dimaio, not as well-known as the others, and in practice for just eight years, objected to the approach of the more seasoned attorneys and stood his ground.

Dimaio disagreed with the strategy and followed his own counsel. Throughout the trial, DiMaio would differentiate himself from the others. Aggressive in his defense, but never crossing any ethical lines. It would be the hallmark of his legal career.

Dimaio said, "I represent my client diligently and thoroughly within the canon of ethics, no more and no less. I take my obligations to that seriously."

For DiMaio, an aggressive defense does not require knowingly perjured testimony or underhanded tactics. He put his effort into using every aspect of the law and trial procedure to expose the flaws in the government's case and rely on the jury to recognize reasonable doubt. As it turned out, his approach was both ethical and successful.

In a criminal trial, discovery works in two directions. By filing for access to the prosecution's case, Flynn would have to disclose his own witnesses, the others would not yet benefit from seeing the government's case. Flynn's lawyer did precisely that, providing the name of their one witness.

Dimaio remembers the pre-trial discussions.

"Harvey Brower wanted to put witnesses on the stand that I knew, in my opinion, were not telling the truth and had nothing to do with Jerry's defense whatsoever.

"Some of the other defendants decided that I was going to be the one to present these witnesses.

"In a meeting at the prison with Jerry and myself, I told him first that I wasn't going to do that and then I told the other defendants with their counsel present that I wasn't going to do it.

"I told them that I would withdraw before putting someone on the stand that I know was a perjurer. Especially more so when it has nothing to do with my case, and I don't know who they are.

"After that meeting, the decision was to be made by the other defendants and their attorneys as to whether or not I continued. If I stayed, it would only be in our manner in representing Mr. Tillinghast. Mr. Tillinghast and I would take no directions from the other defendants and the defendants' lawyers.

"Having said that, Mr. Tillinghast stood up and said that he would handle the case himself without a lawyer before Mr. DiMaio is asked to do something he is not comfortable with. I then left.

"When I came back a couple of days later, it was determined that I would do Mr. Tillinghast alone and that the other lawyers would stop trying to ask me to put certain witnesses on that were not our witnesses. We proceeded from there.

"If I remember correctly, there was one witness that took the stand, I think Mr. Brower had him on, that never came back for cross-examination. His testimony was stricken. We used to joke and say that Harvey Brower has 'the Boston witness pool.' He would bring them in at different trials."

This element of Brower's approach to trial might explain his later disbarment. Yet for this trial, Brower embraced the strategy.

Flynn's testimony would make for some exciting exchanges in the court. Ultimately it would fail because of the perceptive analysis of DeRobbio's assistant prosecutor, John Murphy, and the street smarts and persuasiveness of the investigators.

But all this was yet to come.

Picking the Jury

Jury selection is one of the most critical aspects of any criminal trial. When organized crime casts its dark shadow over a case, it becomes more complicated. Add in the one degree of separation that is the State of Rhode Island and finding an impartial jury is damn near impossible.

The defense must weed out those victimized by the mob, and the prosecution must look for hidden relationships. The mob mystique, and the 'I know a guy' undercurrent that is Rhode Island, make for a daunting task.

The pool of jurors was the largest ever assembled for a criminal case. Jury selection began on April 12, 1976, and took six weeks. While jury selection is rarely exciting, the nature of the case and the defendants involved made for tumultuous moments.

Jerry recalls someone got their hands on a "blue book," an information resource back before the age of Google used by the police to locate people.

Like a telephone book on steroids.

"They were looking for connections to the people on the jury list, someone they could get to. We were fighting for our freedom, that's all that mattered to us. The cops and prosecutors would do whatever they could to twist the jury their way, we were doing the same thing."

On the second day of jury selection, the judge denied a defense counsel motion regarding the presence of armed uniformed state troopers in the courtroom. This decision would play a key role in Jerry's future. The politics of the Attorney General's office, something as benign as professional jealousy, would start a sequence of events no one could foresee at the time.

The defense argued the mere presence of the armed troopers prejudiced the jury. Judge Giannini denied the motion citing security concerns by the Superintendent of the State Police, Colonel Walter Stone. The troopers would stay.

While the presence of the troopers may have offered a sense of security to the jury and other in the courtroom, what it did not do was intimidate the defendants. With twelve jurors and four alternates selected for the panel, the trial was set to begin, and the antics of the defendants escalated.

A second motion by the defense, to restrict the mention of the Patriarca name by the prosecution witnesses, received a more favorable decision by the judge. The mere mention of Patriarca's name, in the words of the judge, would lend "unwarranted credibility" to hearsay testimony of the witnesses.

Let that sink in for a moment.

The mere mention of Patriarca's name would make customarily excluded and unreliable hearsay testimony credible. It is one of the many 'incredible' examples of Patriarca's influence in Rhode Island. Permeating even into the criminal courts.

The defense and prosecution reached an accommodation on the name. Any references to Patriarca will be masked as John Doe, Sr. Or Jr.

Only in Rhode Island could "you know who" play such a big

part in a criminal case. And you can hide them behind any pseudonym you like, everyone knew who they were.

Trial Antics

During the run-up to the trial, a fight broke out that could mimic a keystone cop movie. There is some conflict as to when, or even if, this altercation took place. Memories have faded over the years, some prefer to forget the past, and some of the participants are no longer alive.

As best as can be put together, the incident happened during a preliminary hearing. Long before the jury was selected.

The exact cause of the melee remains unknown, but here is Jerry and Attorney Paul Dimaio's version.

During the proceedings, there had been four uniformed state troopers, two deputy sheriffs and six marshals in the courtroom. The troopers were armed with shotguns and sitting in the front row. Observing in court on that day was a group of students.

"I'm sitting in behind Paul DiMaio, my attorney. Directly to his right is the assistant prosecutor, John Murphy. Directly to his right is Albert DeRobbio."

Jerry believed Murphy was glancing at DiMaio's notes. During a break, Jerry told him that he wanted to sit next to him to block the prosecutor from reading them. Dimaio agreed. During the next break, Jerry stood up and began speaking to DiMaio. A deputy sheriff approached and tried to put cuffs on Jerry.

"I said, wait a minute! I'm talking to my lawyer. He puts the handcuffs on me and a state trooper, the biggest trooper I ever saw, squeezed my wrist. This was a big man. 'Squeeze a little harder I said I think I'm gonna cum' and I spit in his face. The four troopers armed with shotguns and the others jerked their heads back. I didn't give a fuck. They were trying to take my life away. I didn't give a fuck about them. A struggle started, and we were all trying to get the fuck outta there. A shorter state trooper, I think he was wearing sergeant's stripes, tried to hit me from behind. I said, 'You little weasel. Why don't you come downstairs, so I can beat your fuckin brains in and bring your gun, so I can stick it up your ass and empty it you piece of shit."

The fight happened in a small area of the courtroom and chairs were flying everywhere. During the struggle, Tillinghast's lawyer found himself under a pile of swinging fists. The visiting kids were cheering, but Jerry later apologized for the language.

There was another memorable moment during the trial concerning prosecutor Albert DeRobbio, whose father had just died.

Jerry remembers the moment well.

"I said, 'Hey you motherfucker, I'm gonna get acquitted in this trial, and when I do I'm gonna dig up your dead father and throw him on your fuckin' lawn you fuckin' punk.' He was foaming at the mouth."

DiMaio said of DeRobbio, "That was his M.O. He would whisper terrible things under his breath, hoping to spark a display of temper."

Jerry insists the police were trying to kill him and the others by leaving the keys in the door to the cell in the holding area.

"The sheriff brought us downstairs, and the window next to our cells was wide open. Then I noticed the keys left in the door. I pointed it out to Chucky. I said, 'those motherfuckers are trying to kill us.'

"I yelled for the marshal and told him to lock the door. There was no doubt in my mind we were set up to escape and be shot.

The place was surrounded by SWAT teams. That's another reason I knew they were losing their case. That's how dirty them motherfuckers are."

At one point, the defense wanted a recess but didn't think the judge would grant it. Jerry, after listening to the lawyers' discussion, stood up in the courtroom and told the judge his life was threatened by two troopers. He identified them as Tony Mancuso and Mike Urso.

Jerry told the judge the troopers said they would get him in a dark alley.

"Boy, if looks could kill, I was dead." Jerry chuckled. "Mancuso would have strangled me with his bare hands in front of the jury if he could."

The judge warned the troopers and prosecutor not to speak to the defendants, but Jerry got the continuance.

There were several bomb threats during the trial, all causing more delays. Jerry contends the troopers did it. The troopers denied they were responsible. The circus was in town, and the show was going to be memorable.

"I believed at the time that the court was like an arena," Jerry says. "That was my way of describing it. I didn't fight with the cops when they came to arrest me. I'd just say, see you in the arena. I think that's why they were so set on getting me. Because we, Paul and I, kept beating them in the arena."

Jerry smiles. "Look, you can't go in there and tell the truth all the time. The truth is so bizarre, nobody believes it. Whoever lies the best most of the time gets off. Sometimes they believe the cops, sometimes they believe us. It's not what most people think it is and the cops, the judges, and the prosecutors all know it. They got all the power, we had to do what we could to level the playing field."

Jerry's take on the realities of the courtroom was not all that self-serving. His opinion puts him in agreement with some respected legal company.

Famed lawyer Alan M. Dershowitz, in his book *The Best Defense*[19], offers thirteen rules of the justice game.

"Rule I: Almost all criminal defendants are, in fact, guilty.

Rule II: All criminal defense lawyers, prosecutors, and judges understand and believe Rule I.

Rule III: It is easier to convict guilty defendants by violating the Constitution than by complying with it, and in some cases it is impossible to convict guilty defendants without violating the Constitution.

Rule IV: Almost all police lie about whether they violated the Constitution in order to convict guilty defendants.

Rule V: All prosecutors, judges, and defense attorneys are aware of Rule IV.

Rule VI: Many prosecutors implicitly encourage police to lie about whether they violated the Constitution in order to convict guilty defendants.

Rule VII: All judges are aware of Rule VI.

Rule VIII: Most trial judges pretend to believe police officers who they know are lying.

Rule IX: All appellate judges are aware of Rule VIII, yet many pretend to believe the trial judges who pretend to believe the lying

---

[19] Dershowitz, Alan M. The best defense. 1. Trials -- United States. 2. Dershowitz, Alan M. I. Title. KF220.D37 1983 345.73'02 82-40426e ISBN: 978-0-307-75520-9 347.3052 v3.1

police officers.

Rule X: Most judges disbelieve defendants about whether their constitutional rights have been violated, even if they are telling the truth.

Rule XI: Most judges and prosecutors would not knowingly convict a defendant who they believe to be innocent of the crime charged (or a closely related crime).

Rule XII: Rule XI does not apply to members of organized crime, drug dealers, career criminals, or potential informers.

Rule XIII: Nobody really wants justice."

In the arena, the rules are different. But the courtroom did little to intimidate Jerry. He had confidence in his lawyer, Paul Dimaio, and wasn't afraid to fight for himself.

Jerry recalled an incident during the trial where he refused to be brought to court until he had the proper tie for his suit.

"My wife, Terri, brought one of my suits to the prison, but she brought the wrong tie. It didn't match. I refused to put it on and wanted to wait until she brought the right one."

The marshal said, 'you aren't waiting, let's go.' I laughed, we were all in there, all the Bonded Vault defendants, and the marshal thought he'd intimidate me.

I smiled at him. Look, I said, I ain't going nowhere, take the others and come back for me. You think you can do something different, go ahead and try.

There was a guard there who was in charge of the inmates' clothes. He was a good guy. We used to play gin rummy together when he first started. I usually beat him, and he'd have to do pushups. Whenever I lost, I did sit-ups because of my wrist.

It would be funny because everybody would be quiet and all you could hear was his keys banging on the cement floor when he did his pushups.

Anyway, he says 'leave him here, it's not worth the argument.'

The marshal took everybody else, then came back for me. When I was brought in the courtroom, Judge Giannini said "Mr. Tillinghast, I understand you refused to be delivered to court this morning with the others. Might I ask why?"

I stood up and said, "Judge, when you get dressed for court your clothes are all laid out, and the tie matches the suit, right?"

"Yes, of course," Giannini said.

"Well, I expect the same thing. I want to show respect for this court. Let's remember here, I am innocent before the court. I don't think it's unreasonable for me to present myself properly dressed before the jury, do you?"

Giannini laughed.

"Fine, Mr. Tillinghast, but please make sure you are ready with the others. We need to move this along."

"I'm sure the marshals hated me for it, but I didn't give a shit. This was my life on trial, and I wasn't gonna let anyone intimidate me."

Dussault Testifies

Once it got underway, the trial testimony painted a frightening picture.

The owner of the Bonded Vault Company was Samuel Levine. It didn't take long after Robert Dussault entered the building at 8:15 a.m. wearing a suit and carrying a briefcase, for Levine to start thinking he was going to die.

Or did it?

Levine testified Dussault, whose name Levine didn't know at the time of the robbery, told him it was a stickup, and if Levine tried to warn anyone by pressing the holdup button, he would blow his head off. Levine testified that he told Dussault that his brothers Hyman and Abraham as well as his sister in law, Rosalind, and secretary Barbara Oliva were also in the building. Dussault forced him to call them to the front one by one.

They were given pillowcases to put over their heads.

The rest of the crew, wearing disguises, entered the building. While they began working to unlock the boxes in the safe, Samuel feared his time might be up. He was the only one who wasn't given a pillowcase to wear. He had been ordered to keep his eyes on the floor but thought the robbers felt he had seen too much.

His secretary, Barbara Oliva, testified another man seemed to be second-in-command. She got a good look at him when he asked if she was OK and lifted the pillowcase. Oliva identified that second man as Charles "Chucky" Flynn. During the trial, when she was on the witness stand, Barbara Oliva pointed out Flynn as the man she had seen on the morning of the robbery.

Dussault was the main show at the trial. He admitted his role in Bonded Vault and testified that he heard about the score from John Ouimette who, he said, learned about it from John Doe, Jr. Aka, Raymond "Junior" Patriarca.

He further testified that he was living with Chucky Flynn at 5 Golf Avenue in East Providence when they got a visit from John Ouimette with information about a good score.

Dussault told the court that, in exchange for his testimony, the state had promised him he wouldn't go to jail for this crime or any other crime he might have committed in Rhode Island and would help him in other cases he had against him in Massachusetts.

He described how plans were hatched at a house Flynn had rented in East Providence at 5 Golf Avenue. He had moved there to live with Flynn and Flynn's girlfriend. Dussault detailed the planning and execution of the robbery, his fleeing to Las Vegas, the encounter with Flynn and the others, and the police lying to him about Flynn being dead.

The Attorney General's office kept their end of the bargain going so far as to have a state prosecutor represent Dussault at his court appearances on criminal charges in Massachusetts.

A promise is a promise.

Dussault wouldn't be the only participant to testify.

Joe "the Dancer" Danese once told Flynn, "I'm not going to jail for this motherfucker...," talking about Dussault when Flynn decided not to kill him in Vegas. He kept his word when he decided to cooperate.

In the book, *The Last Good Heist,* Tim White details some background information on Danese's road from Bonded Vault robber and almost hit man to cooperating witness.

"Danese decides he wants to turn state's evidence, but he's no dummy. He knows he can't just up and do it unless he wants to spend the rest of his days with a target on his back. He needs permission, which means he needs to deal with the man in The Office on Federal Hill. So, he calls, talks to one of Patriarca's top men, Henry Tameleo or Nicky Bianco, sources say, and explains his problem.

Danese says he is told, "Sure. None of these guys matter to us, none of them. But you've got to do one thing. If anybody takes the stand and says anything that looks like it's going to be a threat to us, you've got to testify to just the opposite, you've got to contradict them. Capisce?[20]*"*

---

[20] The Last Good Heist: The Inside Story of The Biggest... (n.d.). Retrieved from

Jerry had a different take on that version of Danese decision to cooperate.

"Nothing like that ever happened. Besides Henry was in jail at Walpole, you can check that out. I don't even think that fuckhead Danese would have been able to even talk to him. And Nicky would never do that either.

I would like to know where they got that shit from. Because for my money Danese probably made it up or some old cop's trying to make himself out to have inside info. If he even did contact anybody, whoever that might have been, which I think is bullshit, there's no fucking way that either Henry or Nicky would ever say anything like that.

"You couldn't get Nicky to say three words about anything. He was back and forth to New York, close to Gotti. John and Raymond trusted him completely. If Nicky ever told a rat to testify, they'd have found Nicky in a shallow grave. And Henry, he was starting to show signs of dementia in prison. No way some asshole like Danese reached out to him."

Joe "The Dancer" Danese admitted his role in the robbery and testified against the others. It was a death sentence even if there was any truth to his seeking permission. He and Dussault both entered the Federal Witness Protection Program.

On the date of the robbery, in 1975, Jerry had an alibi. He was at a party with his half-brother, Larry Mastrofine, in New Hampshire. It was Larry who would testify on Jerry's behalf at the trial.

It is another interesting story on how Jerry found out he had

---

https://www.goodreads.com/book/show/28646699-

the-last-good-heist

a half-brother named Larry.

Jerry recalls the incident.

"I was working with my father at the time. I owned this red Corvair in excellent condition. I parked it on a side street.

"One day, I went to get the car, and it was gone. Pissed me off. Sometime later, I was driving with my father on Atwells Avenue, and I spotted someone parking my car.

"I yelled for my father to stop and ran over to the car. As the guy got out, I started slapping the shit out of him.

'You stole my fuckin' car, you asshole.'

"He was begging me to stop. 'I didn't know it was yours' he said. My father came over and told me to stop.

'You can't hit him,' he told me.

'Why not?' I asked.

'He's your brother.'

"I was stunned for a moment. Then I said, "is there anybody else out there I need to know about? My father just smiled and walked away."

Despite the rancor of their initial meeting, blood is indeed thicker than water. Larry testified for Jerry.

Some of the prosecution witnesses actually helped, more than hurt, Jerry's case.

Dussault, the star witness for the prosecution, wasn't all that helpful to the state's case against Jerry. Danese wasn't any better, and none of the employees ever got a look at anyone other than Dussault and Flynn.

"He (Dussault) couldn't even pronounce my fucking name. He kept calling me Tillingham, Tillinghate... I knew him as Chucky's friend."

DeRobbio kept trying to help Dussault get the name right, emphasizing Jerry's name with each question. Dimaio objected.

The Judge sustained the objection, ruling DeRobbio was leading the witness.

DeRobbio's attempt to rehabilitate the witness failed in the jury's eyes. His efforts were to no avail.

Larry's testimony about Jerry was all it took to convince the jury.

But the biggest event in the defense case was some clever trial tactics that might have sowed the seeds of reasonable doubt had the prosecution fallen for it.

When the state recovered the stolen van used in the robbery, they recovered human pubic hair. FBI analysis determined the hair belonged to a black individual, a Negroid male in the vernacular of the day, based on the best available technology of the day. The defense plan called for Flynn to take the stand and his lawyer asking two questions.

When the prosecution rested, the defense started in. After the usual round of motions to dismiss were denied, they put Flynn on the stand.

John F. 'Jack' Cicilline, representing John Ouimette, did the questioning.

> Cicilline: "Mr. Flynn, did you rob Bonded Vault?"
> A. "No"
> Cicilline: "Do you know who did?"
> A. "Yes."
> Cicilline: "No further questions for this witness."

The plan, assuming DeRobbio took the bait, was to blame a black gang out of Atlanta for the robbery. The pubic hair was the proof.

DeRobbio chomped at the bit to go after Flynn, but cooler

more perceptive heads prevailed. Murphy persuaded DeRobbio to ask for a recess. In the hot and oppressive courtroom, any opportunity for a break was welcome. The judge granted the recess, and the prosecution team gathered in a conference room.

A heated discussion took place. DeRobbio wanted to ask Flynn the obvious question, then destroy his credibility. Murphy and Giblin saw the error in this approach. Why even put it out there for the jury to consider? They argued with DeRobbio, finally convincing him to just attack Flynn's credibility with his extensive criminal record and leave the question unasked.

After a few minutes, DeRobbio relented. He'd go after Flynn based on his record and leave the rest alone. As the case played out, it was the right choice.

DeRobbio ignored Flynn's earlier testimony and impeached his credibility by recounting his extensive criminal record, including his escape from a Massachusetts prison.

The defense attorney for Ouimette asked to reopen direct. Giannini denied the motion. He had asked if there were any questions for direct examination by other defense lawyers when Cicilline finished with Flynn, all said no. Giannini ruled it was trial tactics and you'd have to live with it.

Split Decisions

Sequestered for 79 days during the trial and deliberations before handing down its verdict, the jury came up with a split decision.

Three guilty, three not guilty.

John Ouimette, Charles 'Chucky' Flynn, and Ralph 'Skippy' Byrnes were convicted. Jake Tarzian, Walter Ouimette, and Jerry were found not guilty.

The jury was not convinced by Flynn's testimony.

Flynn guilty

Byrnes wife testified he was home with her all day drinking wine. The alibi was broken by Providence Detective Giblin.

Byrnes guilty.

Ouimette coerced a state employee, and auto body shop inspector, to testify he saw Ouimette at an auto body shop on the day of the robbery. He produced a mimeographed copy of records of inspection.

The prosecutors obtained one year of records and noticed a difference between the form in evidence and the other documents produced by the state records. Prosecutors brought in an expert from the mimeograph company to testify that the machine that created the evidence record was not sold to the state until after the trial started. Later investigation determined the employee had feared for his life and that's why he testified.

Ouimette guilty.

Each of the alibis broken by investigators or found not credible by the jury.

When Jerry was arrested for the Bonded Vault case, he had been working as an Environmental Control Inspector for the city of Providence. That job went away. After he was acquitted, the city rehired him as part of the highway department. He eventually became the union steward.

It wasn't so much that Buddy Cianci and the city embraced the concept of innocent until proven guilty. It was more a testament to the influence of the mob and the control they exerted. Jerry got his job back not because of any respect for the law, but because the Mayor needed to keep the union happy.

And the mob was a significant part of the union.

Nicholas Easton, during his time as Providence City Council

President, recalled a meeting with the police chief and the commander of the Providence Police Intelligence Bureau during that period. The commander offered this insight into the highway department.

"We know one-third of the employees are members of organized crime, one-third are associates of organized crime, and the other third does all the work out of fear of organized crime." Pausing for a moment and looking around the room, he added. "And they all vote for the Mayor."

That was Providence in 1976.

Jerry had been so confident of the verdict, he sent his clothes home from the ACI a week before the trial ended. Was it inside information or intuition? Jerry says he just knew the jury believed his alibi and didn't believe Dussault.

"The guy couldn't even get my name right. They could see he was lying."

Once again, Jerry had beaten the odds. His attorney, Paul Dimaio, and the assistant prosecutor, John Murphy, agree on the main reason; they were not able to break Jerry's alibi. Murphy contends it was lack of time and resources, Jerry says it was because it was the truth.

Three men convicted, three found not guilty, and none of the millions in stolen goods ever recovered.

One of the Providence detectives who worked the case had some words with Jerry during the trial.

According to Jerry, "the guy says, Hey Tillinghast, you're going away for a long time. I says I am an innocent man. He yells back, 'if they find you not guilty, I'll give you a blow job on the steps of city hall.' I just laughed about it at the time.

"When the jury came back with a not guilty verdict, a uniform Providence cop came over and asked me how I felt. I smiled and said, 'like a million bucks.' He started yelling and screaming, 'we'll get you next time you son of a bitch.'

Then, I spotted the detective who'd bet I would be convicted. I said, 'Hey, what time you gonna be at city hall, I want to sell tickets to you giving me that blow job? I didn't give a fuck back then. They hated when we won in the arena. It made them more determined to get me, but I didn't give a shit."

While the main tent of the circus was closed, there was one final act by the defense for the three convicted men. It staggers the imagination.

After the conviction, Giannini sentenced the three to life in prison. John Ouimette, Flynn, and Byrnes returned to the ACI to begin their sentence.

John "Jack" Cicilline filed several motions on appeal, including one arguing Judge Giannini had erred by allowing the presence of the shotgun-toting uniformed troopers.

The assistant prosecutor, John Murphy, even all these years later, recalls the incident with barely concealed anger.

"They intentionally went before a particular judge, Florence Murray. I was on vacation, and DeRobbio had already assumed the bench. Another AG, one who did not like DeRobbio and was envious of the trial publicity, appeared for the state. When Cicilline asked for bail pending an appeal to the Supreme Court, the Assistant AG didn't object. I later confronted him, and he said, "It's just a robbery."

In another bizarre twist in a series of strange only-in-Rhode Island twists, three men convicted and sentenced to life in prison for the Bonded Vault case were released on bail. Ouimette and Byrnes returned to the street, Flynn was turned over to Massachusetts authorities since he was an escapee.

Ultimately, Murphy would argue the case all the way to the

United States Supreme Court and get the conviction upheld. Ouimette and Byrnes would remain at large for several years, finally surrendering in 1981 when the state moved to seize the houses and other property of relatives pledged as bail.

Byrnes release and return to Gerard Ouimette's crew would play an integral part in Jerry's next appearance in the arena. One that would send Jerry and his brother Harold to prison for life for killing George Basmajian. Up until now, Jerry has never said anything about that night except one thing.

Harold was an innocent man.

In the forty years that have elapsed since that time, Jerry has never wavered on that one point. But Jerry's loyalty to the code of silence prevented his telling the whole story. The night they were arrested, Jerry told his brother. "You're over twenty-one, man. What can I say? Nothing we can do but go back to the arena."

This time, the arena would be less kind to Jerry and Harold.

But before the story gets to Basmajian, Jerry would be the subject of more intense police interest.

Chapter 11   *A Suspect Once Again*

Imperatore-Lavin Homicide August 1977

Shortly before the Bonded Vault escapade, Jerry was introduced to a tough and formidable guy looking to make his own mark in the dangerous world of organized crime.

George Basmajian, a black belt martial arts expert with the instincts of a street fighter, and Jerry shared similar traits.

Both were fearless. Both found a niche robbing drug dealers. Both were good earners and powerful men, assets in that world.

But they differed in one significant area. Jerry thought things out, Bas could be reckless and impulsive. This recklessness would prove his undoing.

Jerry took a liking to 'Bas' and brought him along when the circumstances dictated a need for his talents. Over the next few years, as Jerry rose in Gerard's organization, Bas would play a part as Jerry's partner in various exploits.

It wouldn't take long for police to suspect the two in a homicide.

Less than a year after his acquittal in the Bonded Vault case, Jerry was back on police radar. In August 1977, two men, Ralph Imperatore and Billy Lavin, left a marina in Warwick.

They were never seen alive again.

According to one former State Police investigator,

"Jerry and George Basmajian were the last two people to see Imperatore and Lavin alive. They grabbed them at the Flying Bridge Marina in Warwick. Imperatore and Lavin had been out on a boat that day. Lavin owned a sailboat. They had a house in Clayville section of Scituate, Rhode Island. They also bought a club called Club Cabaret in Johnston with drug money.

"Tillinghast and Basmajian were showing up at the club, and it looked like they were shaking it down presumably on orders from Gerard because they were part of his crew. Gerard was a powerful criminal because he had put together a crew of tough guys who were loyal and could be trusted. They did everything they were told. Tillinghast was part of that crew. There was another tough guy around called Cesar Ledo who was killed just before George."

The cops would suspect Basmajian in the Ledo homicide, but no charges were ever filed. Some believe the Ledo killing contributed to Gerard's growing concern about Basmajian's recklessness.

If nothing else, it added to the growing interest the cops took in Basmajian and, by association, Jerry. According to Jerry, when another body showed up in Warwick, Warwick police told him to stop dumping bodies in their city. They said to find somewhere else to drop them.

The State Police were a little more persistent, but not any more successful. Whenever the troopers, or any police department for that matter, would grab members of Gerard's crew, they got little cooperation. Gerard and Jerry were from the old school. Admit nothing.

State Police got involved in the Lavin/Imperatore case when Ralph's father, Ralph Imperatore, Sr., filed a complaint with state police on August 13, 1977. He reported his son and a friend, William C. Lavin, missing.

On the evening of August 8, 1977, someone broke into the younger Imperatore's home at Brigadoon Farm, Field Hill Road, in Scituate. The same night Ralph and Billy disappeared.

Imperatore's girlfriend, Francine Doorley, told police about the break-in. She said she went to the home she shared with Imperatore looking for him because he never came back from the marina. She saw two men ransacking the place but was afraid to call the police.

Imperatore's father said his son told him they were being hassled by the Mafia at the club. He also told police a friend of his son's said Ralph, Jr. was in serious trouble and might never be seen again.

These allegations were detailed in an affidavit for a search warrant filed by Vinnie Vespia, at the time a sergeant in the Rhode Island State Police organized crime Intelligence Unit.

Vespia wrote in his affidavit that he interviewed a close friend of Imperatore's who told him of a location behind the Scituate house where a large quantity of money and other items were buried.

The friend went to Imperatore's home on August 10, two days after the victims went missing and said someone had already been digging at the site. The witness reported items were missing.

State Police, armed with a search warrant, went to the scene and began their own digging. They found $120,000 in cash in plastic containers. As part of the investigation, they interviewed people who had been at the marina in the company of Imperatore and Lavin on August 8,1977.

The witnesses reported seeing Jerry Tillinghast and George Basmajian leaving with the missing men. These witnesses further stated that Tillinghast and Basmajian told Imperatore and Lavin that there was trouble at the Club Cabaret and they were needed to be there to straighten it out.

The case against Tillinghast and Basmajian gained strength when Imperatore's girlfriend found a white golf cap on the table in the farmhouse. Witnesses reported Basmajian was wearing a similar hat when he, Jerry, Imperatore, and Lavin were last seen leaving the marina.

According to the search warrant affidavit prepared by Sgt. Vespia, police had grounds to believe Basmajian and Jerry left the marina with the two missing men, drove them to Scituate, forced them to reveal the location of buried money, and killed them.

Police thought two other men, Jerry Christy and Ronald Leone, along with Jerry Tillinghast and George Basmajian, were also involved with the abduction of Lavin and Imperatore.

On the night of their disappearance, witnesses identified all four men at the marina with Lavin and Imperatore. According to state police detectives, both Tillinghast and Basmajian admitted they knew the alleged victims and had been at the Club Cabaret several times.

Jerry Tillinghast and George Basmajian were the main suspects. But without the victims' bodies or other substantial evidence, the case was at a standstill.

Tillinghast said State Police asked him what happened to Lavin and Imperatore. His answer, "How the fuck should I know? Why don't you go to the morgue, pick up two John Doe's and charge me with it? Just don't keep fuckin' with me."

On April 9, 1979, a human skull was found in a yard at 112 Point Avenue, Warwick, Rhode Island, police theorize it had been dug up by a dog.

The following day, on nearby Conimicut Beach, police

removed a concrete slab covering a five-foot deep hole. In the pit, they found the skeletal remains of two men.

One of the bodies was headless, solving the mystery of the skull found nearby. Tests on the remains identified them as 31-year-old William C. Lavin and 28-year-old Ralph R. Imperatore III.

Lavin and Imperatore were drug dealers who had made so much money they needed to find a way to launder it. Buying the Club Cabaret in Johnston gave them a cover to account for the money.

It also made them targets for a mob shakedown.

Robbing drug dealers, according to Jerry, is a perfect crime. "I'd take the money, never the drugs. That'll get you in a big jam. Who's gonna complain? Drug dealers can't go to the cops. I did it because no one gives a fuck what happens to drug dealers. I don't know what happened to Lavin and Imperatore. George never said, and I didn't ask. "

Lavin and Imperatore weren't street level guys. They had worked their way up to a point where they needed to launder large sums of money. Nothing in life is free and, during that time in Rhode Island, one of the costs of the drug business was paying for protection.

The State Police reconstructed the last few hours of the lives of Lavin and Imperatore. It was not a pretty picture.

Lavin owned a boat flying the Jolly Roger pirate flag. He tied it up at the Flying Bridge restaurant at Cowesett Marina. Witnesses said Jerry Tillinghast met him at the marina.

He never seen again.

Shortly after this, Imperatore was seen on the deck at the Marina arguing with his girlfriend, Francine Dooley. She begged him not to go with Tillinghast and Basmajian. Witnesses reported George Basmajian said, "Let's go, Ralph."

145

No one ever saw Imperatore alive again.

Police suspect Jerry, Basmajian, Jerry Christy, and Ronald Leone took Imperatore and Lavin to a location near Imperatore's Scituate home. There they tortured the two in an attempt to find large amounts of hidden cash. Police brought Tillinghast and Basmajian in while the investigation continued. But lack of evidence once again forced the police to release Jerry and George.

Later the same year, Jerry Christy himself would meet a violent end. His body was found stuffed in the trunk of a car. He'd been strangled with a length of piano wire. The usual names arose as suspects, all with links back to Jerry, George, Gerard Ouimette, and Raymond Patriarca.

In October 1979, a Kent County Grand Jury sitting in Warwick indicted Jerry on three charges. One count of conspiracy and two counts of murder.

Imperatore's girlfriend, Francine Doorley, was the principal witness. She would never testify.

On a rain-slicked highway in Pawtucket, Rhode Island, her car skidded out of control and smashed into a tree, killing her. With her death, the Attorney General's office had no choice but to drop the case. Meanwhile, Tillinghast and his brother Harold were doing life in prison for killing Basmajian.

Speculation is always unreliable, but the unlikely coincidence of two suspects in the same homicide dying violently within a short period cannot be ignored. Greed and doubt often trump loyalty and usefulness.

Basmajian's recklessness, and reluctance to give Christy his portion of the loot from the Lavin/Imperatore matter, may have sealed their fate in the eyes of Gerard and Patriarca.

Chapter 12 *Friends and Family*

Friends

To this day people who knew Jerry still talk about him, although not everyone wants their real name used. One of those people requested we use M.B. He was five years old when he first heard about Jerry Tillinghast.

"We lived at 366 Public Street in South Providence, and he was more or less like a big brother." (Jerry was twelve at the time.)

"Our families were very close like a lot of families during that era in South Providence."

M's father was Superintendent of Public Works in Providence for many years, and M worked there for a while. He worked at the Animal Control Office until opening his own business in Cranston which has become very successful. M. Served eighteen years at the Boy's Training School and the Adult Correctional Facility on sexual assault and robbery convictions. He knows the underbelly of society well.

M. does not consider himself a tough guy, but "I didn't give a fuck because people knew I was close to Jerry and I wasn't bullied."

M. remembers a winter storm when Edward "Buckles" Melise, a close ally of Providence Mayor Vincent "Buddy" Cianci, was deputy Superintendent of Public Works and Jerry was a shop steward for the union representing city employees.

"I wasn't getting called in. I had a three-month-old daughter and needed the work. I was on one of the first trucks supposed to be called in, so I called the highway garage, and they told me Buckles called in his own guys."

M. called Michael's Lounge where Jerry could be found most days and told him the story. Jerry immediately called the highway garage for a meeting with Melise and told him to call all the trucks back it. The snow was piling up, and that was the last thing Melise wanted to do. The matter was resolved without incident.

"When Jerry walks into a room, not only does he light up the room, but people light up around him."

After being paroled following nearly 30 years behind bars for the Basmajian murder, Jerry petitioned the parole board to allow him to associate with M. He was initially turned down. A few years later, the board agreed and let the two felons hang out.

"I believe Jerry will never go back to prison," M. said, "he's learned the lesson."

Sometimes, Jerry's friends caused him problems without meaning to.

Between marriages, Jerry lived in several apartments in Providence including one behind Livingston's Bar on Livingston Street in the city's Mount Hope section near the East Side.

Jerry's half-brother Larry, his alibi witness in the Bonded Vault trial, was living in an apartment to the rear of the bar with the owner's son Bob Livingston. Both men had decided to vacate the apartment and offered it to Jerry who found it convenient.

"What they didn't tell me was the apartment had a drop ceiling. I wasn't thinking about looking into the ceiling, who does

148

that? I'm not assuming there is anything in the ceiling."

Jerry was about to discover there was more than empty space in that drop ceiling.

It was a time when police were investigating Jerry's role with George Basmajian in the disappearance of William Lavin and Ralph Imperatore III from a marina in Warwick. Authorities searched Imperatore's property in Scituate. They recovered a significant amount of musty smelling money buried in the yard.

Jerry recalls a state police raid related to that case.

"I'm sitting in a yard about three houses up talking to this young lady. I had a clear view of my apartment. All of a sudden, cop cars pull up. I thought they were raiding Livingston's bar."

Actually, police had a warrant to search Jerry's apartment. Hidden in the drop ceiling, they found gambling slips, two guns, and some bullets that did not match those guns. They also found money on Jerry's bureau he had left there when he went to visit the woman friend.

"I'm watching this and called my lawyer, Paul DiMaio, who went to the scene. When police wanted to know how Paul found out about the raid, he said Jerry told me."

The police were not amused. After Jerry turned himself in, he was charged with possessing gambling slips and weapons. They also confiscated the money which they said had a musty smell.

Jerry's new case went before a no-nonsense judge named Thomas Needham. The same judge, several years later, would preside over the trial of Claus von Bulow. Von Bulow, the Newport socialite, was charged with trying to kill his wife Martha Sunny von Bulow in 1980 by injecting her with insulin.

Von Bulow went on trial for the attempted murder in 1982, making headlines throughout the world as the first to allow cameras in the courtroom. Von Bulow was convicted and sentenced to 30 years in prison. He posted a million dollars bail and remained free pending appeal.

At his second trial in 1985, Von Bulow was acquitted. Needham told the late Channel 12 reporter Glenn Laxton, that when he died the headline would say, "Von Bulow Judge Dies."

He was right, that is precisely what the headline read.

During Jerry's arraignment, Needham told the arresting officers they had basically blown the case of the weapons and money in the drop ceiling. The police had a body warrant to find Jerry, not to search the entire apartment including the drop ceiling. The case was dismissed. Then, Jerry's attorney filed a motion for a return of the money, but not the guns.

The state was ordered to return the money. The guns had been put in the ceiling by half-brother Larry, now deceased, and Bob Livingston, according to Jerry.

They had forgotten about them. When Larry and Bobby realized it, they were too afraid to tell Jerry.

"I would have kicked both their asses."

Family

Jerry and his former wife, Terry, have four children. Jerry, Jr., born 1970, Kristian, born 1972, Jarod, born 1974, and Vanessa, born 1977. A couple of the kids were conceived while Jerry was in prison.

Jerry smiles at the memory.

"Terry would come up to visit me. This was long before the Basmajian case. Someone would distract the guard, and we'd slip off into the bathroom and take care of business. Made the time a little easier and my life a whole bunch better when the kids came

150

along." He pauses a moment to gather his thoughts.

"Even when I was in prison, I stayed involved in my kids' lives. I had to. Terry had issues with alcohol and drugs, she wasn't the most consistent mother. My sister, Helen 'Sissy', had the kids most of the time. But I had ways of staying involved. I had eyes on the street. If they screwed up, I knew about it. I made sure they kept their noses clean as much as any parent could."

One thing is readily apparent when you speak with Jerry's children. While each has mixed memories of growing up under the shadow of a father in prison, they all agree their father worked hard at keeping them in line.

Somehow, despite being in prison here and out of state, Jerry found a way to be in their lives.

Helen 'Sissy' Tillinghast Pirri

Helen Tillinghast Pirri, known as Sissy, is Jerry's younger sister and named after their mother, Helen. She has always been one of Jerry's strongest supporters.

When Jerry was on trial in the Bonded Vault case Helen, then just a teenager, led a protest outside the Providence Superior Court against what she perceived as unfair treatment of the defendants by the court.

Always there to help, she ended up raising Jerry's and Harold's kids after the brothers were convicted.

"When Jerry went away and had problems with Terry, I took care of his kids and basically raised them as if they were my own kids. I helped with Harold's kids, too."

"Throughout my life, I've always had some of my family members living with me and taking care of them. Your family is the most important thing. That is why I took them in. I didn't want them to be misplaced. I wanted them to be in a family environment, to see their father.

They would go to their mom on weekends, and they would be wild. After the weekend I would get them home and get them readjusted again when could take two or three days. I would just situate them back to their routine, and she'd (Terry) want them back again."

She recalls some difficult moments over the years.

"Lots of times I had a bunch of personalities here. I was 25 years old. I had seven kids, and five weren't mine."

Gerry Jr.

Gerald M. Tillinghast Jr. is Jerry first son. He spells his name with a G, Gerry, to differentiate himself from his father.

But changing a letter cannot conceal a legacy.

His life lies in the shadow of the other Jerry Tillinghast. For a time, Gerry went by a different name. But the family resemblance and the insular community that is Rhode Island made the effort fruitless.

Gerry was nine years old when his father went to prison for the Basmajian murder, but he'd been in and out for as long as Gerry could remember.

"Almost the very next day, when he went away for good, friends weren't my friends anymore. 'Your dad's a murderer,' they said. It was rough. What could I do? I was nine. All I knew is he was my dad, and now he was gone."

Life at home became turmoil.

"My mom struggled with alcohol and drugs. Once my father went to prison, it got worse. She'd be drinking a beer while we were heading off to school and be drunk when we got home.

152

"My dad was strict with us. He'd find out about something we did, or problems with our schoolwork, and try to punish us by making us stay in.

"Mom would just agree with him on the phone, then let us do whatever we wanted. It wasn't a good time. At some point, my mother just gave up arguing with my dad. We were shuffled off to relatives. My Aunt Helen, everybody called her Sissy, played a big part in raising us."

Gerry recalls the prison visits and seeing his father with all the other inmates, the ones with the special privileges.

"It wasn't a prison for a certain group of guys, and my father and Uncle Harold were part of that group. My dad called us every night. We'd wait for the call, and he would talk to us all. It never occurred to me that he was any different than the other inmates but, as I got older, I could see the guards and other prisoners treated him, and us, differently."

For Gerry, his whole world changed.

"Everything in the bucket just pours out and goes everywhere. Some of that you never find again.

"The worst part is being judged without ever having done anything. You shouldn't judge a book by its cover. Just because the cover is withered, it might have a story behind it. The chapters inside may not be as withered."

The cover of Gerry's book was the Tillinghast name and all that entailed.

He will be the first to admit it was not without benefits.

"Where we lived, the name was a legend. Some privileges went with it. There was envy from others, resentment from a few. People would trip over themselves to be a small part of it.

"They expected me to be a certain way, I found that out quickly. The minute I got my license and could get around, I found that out."

Just before he turned eighteen, Gerry and his friends had been looking forward to invading the club scene. It was not to be, the law changed, and he'd have to wait three more years.

"I was pissed, but I also knew there was another way. My dad was always talking about his friends and the clubs they owned. I paid attention.

"I'd put on a suit, I'd always wear a suit. It projects a particular image. I'd go to the club, and the bouncer would say, 'You got an Id?'

"I'd asked if the owner was there. Tell him Jerry Tillinghast Jr. is at the door. They take me in the back, and I'd tell the owner, 'Look, my dad doesn't have a problem with me being here if you don't have a problem with it.'

"Like magic, they'd let me into the club. And man, once the women knew who I was, well... let's just say it was a crazy time.

"The next thing you know, it's one thing after another. Before you know it, you're wrapped up into a system you had no intention of getting into in the first place."

Gerry met a seventeen-year-old girl, and they had a son. It was not destined to be a long-term relationship, their lives complicated by the woman's heroin addiction.

A short time after that relationship soured, Gerry met his wife. They've been married twenty-five years and have three children.

By his own admission, the first five years of marriage was hell for his wife.

"I was never home. I was involved in running drugs. I wasn't doing what I should be doing. At some point, I realized this had to stop. I didn't know where it would lead me, but I knew it wouldn't end well."

Gerry now has a degree from Johnson and Wales University for Computer-aided Drafting and Culinary Arts. He's always had an eye for art. He tried to further his education at RIC (Rhode Island

College), but he suffers from a hearing deficit. He had difficulty hearing the lectures.

"My father wanted me to go to RISD (Rhode Island School of Design), but I turned him down. Art was a big part of my life when I was growing up.

"One time, I did a portrait of my mother. I worked on it for months. My mother was a beautiful woman, I'd captured that beauty in the drawing.

"Come to the end of school, awards are given out for art and other things. I'm up on stage to receive my award and no one, not one family member, is there to see it.

"I threw the portrait in the trash and never looked back."

Even with the degree and skills that go with it, it's still not enough to get him out from the Tillinghast shadow.

"The worst thing for me, being an educated man, was the first question they always asked. 'Are you related to Jerry and Harold?'

"They knew, but they wanted to hear it.

"This was always followed by, Oh, that's interesting. Your resume is in order, everything looks good. We'll call you."

"The call never came."

Gerry, like his brother and sisters, has a good relationship with his father.

"We talk all the time. Sometimes my dad shares old stories, and I listen. We get along great now."

To a certain extent, the Jerry Tillinghast of the past has faded from history. The revived interest in the cases he is associated with, sparked by the Crimetown podcast and books on the Bonded Vault case, stimulated a whole new generation's curiosity about those times.

For Gerry, while the intensity of the name may have faded, the shadow never did. To lessen the effect, he surrounds himself with people he considers true friends, not sycophants for the allure of organized crime.

"The friends I have now know me as Gerry. They don't care about the Tillinghast part. The things that matter now are my family and those good friends.

"I'm glad my dad is out. I'm happy I have time to spend with him away from the prison environment. People need to understand the realities of organized crime, and the cost to families.

"When I was growing up, I wanted to be a cop. I wanted to destroy organized crime. To take from them what they took from me. Organized crime took my father, they took my family, they took my childhood, and, for the longest time, they controlled my life even though I wasn't part of it.

"Listen, it ain't the Sopranos or Goodfellas. The image most people have about organized crime is bullshit.

"It's not about loyalty.

"It's not about honor.

"It's not about the family.

"It's about greed and treachery and manipulation. It tears the real family apart for the sake of a false one.

"My family paid a big price for being associated with that life. We all had to find our own way to cope. I lived it. It wasn't anything like TV or the movies.

"Anybody who thinks differently never spent a moment in my world."

Jarrod

Jarrod Tillinghast is Jerry's youngest son. Born in 1974 Jarrod was four years old when Jerry went to prison.

"My first memory is fuzzy, but I remember a lot of police lights and chaos when my mother shot him," recalling the night his mother put a round in his father's knee.

After that, it was prison visits and the mixed emotions of seeing his father and having to leave him when the time was up.

"It was always a mix of excitement and dread. Excited to see my dad. To talk with him about things and dreading when I'd have to leave.

"There's a yellow line you cross in the visiting area. Once you cross that line, it's over. I remember how sad I was when my father and the other inmates would head back.

"I'd be standing on the other side of the yellow line, and the visit was over. That's what stands out in my mind."

Like his siblings, Jarrod knew his father was an attentive dad no matter if he was locked up.

"He had eyes on the street, and he was always on the phone with my aunt or others. If I was supposed to be home at 5 and walked in at 5:01 it was a week in the house. No friends. No going anywhere. Each minute late cost me a week."

Jarrod bore the Tillinghast name as best he could. He never used it to his advantage and tried to avoid the usual disadvantages.

"I can remember, even as a young kid before I was able to drive, getting stopped by the cops. As soon as they heard the name they'd drag us out of the car. I got used to it.

"But I would tell everybody I have a first name before my last name. I'm not my father. I wanted to be Jarrod, not just Jerry Tillinghast's son."

As a young boy, Jarrod had the good fortune to live near a Rhode Island State Trooper, now retired Lieutenant Robert 'Bobby' Magnan. The Lieutenant, a young trooper at the time, and his wife took a liking to Jarrod and, with his mother's consent, would take him to various places.

"He's a good-hearted kid," Lieutenant Magnan said. "When he was with us, I didn't let the command staff of the State Police know about it. They'd have probably not looked kindly on it, which was unfair to Jarrod. He was just a kid then. He made some bad decisions in his life, but he's learned from those mistakes."

He recalls another connection to Jarrod that happened long after the days when he was just a small boy.

"In the close-knit world of Rhode Island, after Jarrod was a grown man, he was sitting in the bar at Venda and struck up a conversation with my son. They've since become close friends."

Jarrod fondly recalls the time he spent with Lieutenant Magnan and his wife.

"They didn't care who my father was. They just wanted me to have fun once in a while. I will always be thankful for that."

As to the bad decisions Magnan mentioned, Jarrod uses the same words about his life as his father does.

"I made my own choices, and I lived with the consequences."

Jarrod is built like a truck, and his athletic ability led him into sports and, eventually, into boxing. He can remember his father, whenever he had a furlough, coming to his football games.

"It meant a lot to me. He was trying to stay involved, trying to keep tabs on us. He was very involved in everything; school, sports, knowing who I was hanging out with, all of that."

Boxing was his way to opportunity. From a piece by Tim Stuby called *Name of the Father* on the victory journal website. (https://victoryjournal.com/stories/name-of-the-father/)

"Boxing changed my life," he (Jarrod) says. "When I started fighting I wasn't a loose cannon anymore." This isn't to say he became an altar boy. He still went out with the fellas. Still managed to mix it up on the streets. But he'd turned a corner. "I was proud of him," says his father."

Jarrod's success in the amateur ring and his wins at Golden Glove matches launched a career in the pro circuit. After boosting the training to a new level with the help of local promoter Jimmy Burchfield and former pro boxer Dino Denis, by 1999 Jarrod rolled up a 7-0 record.

All that changed one rainy night in June 2000 on Route 37 in Cranston Rhode Island. Ironically, just one exit before the one his father took that fateful night he was arrested for murder.

Jarrod's Cherokee Jeep was rear-ended by a truck. His left elbow was shattered in the accident. His boxing career derailed.

What followed was surgery, bad decisions, dabbling in crime, and lost opportunities.

In the same article Stuby writes,

"Despite his laughter and indefatigable optimism, Jarrod can't fully mask tinges of regret. The choices made. The haunting vestiges of what might have been. A deadly puncher. He could have been a franchise. His people didn't care what ticket prices were, they wanted to see him. You don't have that with a lot of fighters."

All that is past now. Divorced and often entangled in the

murky, complicated, and confusing web of domestic relation nightmares, Jarrod looks to the future and the bright spot of his two children.

"Some of the things I got charged with; violating no-contact orders by talking to my children, text messages about gifts, were bullshit. If my last name hadn't been Tillinghast, it wouldn't have gone anywhere. But it is what it is. Now I just focus on my business and my kids."

And of course, the business involves boxing. *Brawl for it All*, an exciting concept where street grudges, the kind where people often get hurt, locked up, or killed, are settled in the controlled violence of a boxing ring.

It has grown exponentially and looks to lead to great things for Jarrod.

As for his own sons, he'd prefer boxing not be a choice.

"If they show an interest, I'll teach them the skills of boxing, but I don't want to see them taking punches in the ring. I'll support them in whatever they choose, but I'd discourage that."

And for his relationship with his father?

"Things are good. We have a great relationship. He's my dad and no matter what he will always be part of my life."

Kristian

Kristian (Tillinghast) Ferland, Jerry's first daughter, talked about her memories of growing up.

"I remember waiting for him to come home from work. I was four or five-years old. He worked at the Shipyard in Providence, I think. We'd wait for him to come home. It was just a normal life. I remember my mother drinking a lot. Her and my father would argue.

160

One time, he had been away for a few days. I guess they'd argued. He came in, and my mother started yelling at him. We were all around, all the kids. Next thing I knew, my mother shot my dad in the leg. My Uncle John came over and then the cops. It was crazy.

There were always lots of my father's friends around, and my uncles. I remember Gerard and Johnny Ouimette being over the house. I loved both of them. They were always nice to me. I never knew them as anything other friends of my dad."

Kristian recalled difficult times between her mother and father. "My mother drank a lot and used drugs. I have a lot of anger from those days. I've come to terms with it, but the memories are painful.

I remember the day I found out my dad wasn't coming home. I couldn't understand why. He was my dad, and he was always there."

She fought back the tears.

"I remember going to the prison to see him. I hated going there because I wanted my dad to be home with me."

One poignant memory has always stuck with her.

"For Valentine's Day, I made a ceramic heart for my father. He was in maximum security at the time. As I was walking up the stairs with my mother, I tripped and dropped the heart. Every few steps I'd trip. The heart ended up in pieces. I was devastated, but my mother just laughed. She wasn't very good for us when we were growing up. I've told her this. I know she's my mom, but she wasn't a good one.

"Anyway, by the time I got to see my dad the heart was in several pieces. It didn't matter to my dad. He acted like it was the best present he ever got. That's how I remember growing up. My dad was always involved in our lives. I could talk to him about anything. Sometimes I think he was shocked at the things I would ask about. He'd tell me to talk to my aunt. But whenever he could, he gave me the best advice. Like most kids, when I got into my teens, I got a little rebellious, but somehow my dad always found a way to keep tabs on me."

She recalled one stark reminder of the realities of her father's living conditions. Right around the time of her thirteenth birthday, she happened to turn on the TV when a news story came on about her father being stabbed in prison.

"Here I was all excited about becoming a teenager, and suddenly my father is on TV surrounded by prison guards. I saw a huge bandage on his shoulder. I didn't know if he was going to live or not. My mother never tried to warn me about the incident, never tried to explain it before I saw the news. It scared me to think of losing him."

Later, when she had her own kids, she says she tried to cushion the realities of their grandfather being in prison.

"I learned from my father to just face up to the realities. I explained to them as best they could understand at their age why the grandfather was there. As they got older, they became more curious."

She recalled an incident one day when one of her kids came home from school.

"Ma, I was bored in school today."

She asked, with a bit of trepidation, what he'd done.

"I Googled Grandpa."

"Oh boy," she said." Well, you'll have to talk to him about that."

How about the growing up Tillinghast part? How did that affect her life?

Kristian chuckled. "There three kind of reactions when

162

people learned my name and who my father was. First, it was oh my god stay away. The second was, do you know who her father is? And third, it was parents steering their kids away. I didn't have many friends, but I have a small group of friends who have stayed with me since we first met. To them, my dad was just my dad. They didn't care about where he was or what anyone said about him.

" That's the way it is between my dad and me. He's my dad, and that's all I care about. Everything else doesn't matter. He's never tried to hide the things he's done. He's always been upfront and said he made some bad choices and paid the price. But he's still my dad. He's my rock. That's all that matters to me. Some people think I have tunnel vision about my dad. I guess that's right, but I don't care."

She never listened to the Crimetown podcast in which her father played such a significant part. Never paid much attention to the newspaper or TV stories.

"One thing I can say as proof of how my dad stayed involved and kept us kids mostly in line. When you consider the circumstances we all grew up in, the fact that we've stayed away from any serious trouble and have survived is all you need to know. When he couldn't be there in person, he made sure someone was. While he isn't perfect, he was a more concerned and involved father than many of the people I know who never were in prison.

"When he came home, it was like he'd never left. There was no catching up, no filling in the years, he already knew it all."

Vanessa

Vanessa is the youngest of the Tillinghast children. She was born in 1977 so by the time she was barely two-years-old, her father was serving a life sentence. She reflects on her memories of growing up.

"I remember always wondering why he was in jail? What he did wrong? Why no one ever told me anything I asked about? Why was I always with my godfather and not my actual father?

"I loved being with my godfather, Gary 'Tiger' Balletto. He was my everything back then. My godfather was the best for the job and believe me I never felt unloved.

"He treated me like a little princess. Spoiled me and my godmother did too. Not the godmother I was baptized with (she passed when I was 2) my aunt Pinky. She took the responsibility of being my godmother.

"I don't remember being with anyone else really. Up until my godfather got sick with cancer did my little world start to crumble. I spent most of my time and visits with my father, with my godfather, and my Uncle John. I was closest to them two. My godfather died when I was 8.

"It still feels like he died yesterday but I recently dealt with the emotional aspect about a year ago. Much easier now to deal with. Now I can miss godfather and talk about him and not get upset."

How about growing up with a dad in prison?

"Well growing up for me was a visiting room with coloring books, playing with my siblings or cousins either inside the prison or out in the prison yard.

"I was the youngest girl so I would get pushed aside because the older ones hogged up the visit with all their shenanigans. Who wasn't listening to which adult or acting up or fighting blah blah blah.

"Then, at about 9, I started speaking up about being left out, and dad changed that. They used to get mad because I was the baby."

What about growing up Tillinghast? Did the name cause problems?

"Well, I had my share of bullshit having Tillinghast for my last name. Problems with jobs, cops, and stuff. But my older siblings threw their name around. I never did that.

"Not ever.

"Everything I am, everything I had and worked for was because of me. Not my dad or our family name. Besides, I'm not that type of person.

"You know my dad had lots and lots of time to be a super dad from behind bars. Not being at all disrespectful, but we were definitely closer mentally than we were when he got out.

"The first time he was closer to me and my sister. Then he went back in, came out, and was close to my brothers. It was weird. Him and I fought a lot, and I mean we went at it.

"I just felt like he owed us time.

"We devoted our life visiting him, and it was not being returned and I was pissed.

"There were things that I looked forward to my whole life that he didn't want to do, and I was not accepting that until I just came to terms with that's who he is, and I can't change him.

"No one can.

"But now we have been fine for a long time. It's been a couple of years now where we stopped arguing and just came to terms with one another's differences.

"We are okay now.

"My mother struggled with alcohol and drug issues. It was inevitable this would affect us kids. But my mother is my mother. Good, bad, or indifferent, I love that woman.

"Yes, my mother's drug and alcohol habit made our life more problematic than it had to be. I practically raised my four youngest siblings and bounced around from family to family because my mom was unstable. There was a lot of violence in the home, and we were all fortunate to have a family to take us in.

"However, it was always made clear how Jerry's kids were the burden to everyone else and believe me as bad as it was at my mother's, there was no place in the world I'd rather be than with my mother. I was welcomed, loved unconditionally, and no one treated me like mom did except Uncle Gary and Aunt Pinky.

"There was nothing like it.

"As I grew and started to have my own family, I knew what I didn't want; no violence, no drugs, no instability. I met my Pedro at 17 and got pregnant 3 months later. Dad wanted me to have an abortion. Because I was so young, he asked me if I thought I'd be with Pedro in two years? I said don't know and don't care. I'll do it alone. I had my son Enrique, and a week later I was on my own. I never looked back.

"Twenty-four years later, here we are. Pedro and me. Two kids, Enrique is now twenty-three and Alyssiana, my daughter, is 18. I'm a great mother. Lord knows I'm not a perfect mother, but I'm a great one. You know if it wasn't for all the shit I've been through in my life with my mother I wouldn't be the mother or wife I am today.

"Just like my dad, I had to come to terms with the fact that my mom had a rotten life with her mother. And she did what she knew...and she did her best even though it could have been 1000 percent better. I knew she loved me. She always wanted me. I learned from both my parents. Dad was there mentally. Mom was their physically. I made it. A little crazy but I'm here living my life and loving it

"My husband and I are in love. We have the best friendship anyone could ever have. Have two spoiled brats, and I couldn't have asked for a better life. I have no regrets."

How does Wicca play a part in her life?

"I've always been into it. Tarot cards, psychics. I've seen things in my life that were calling to me.

"I spent most of my adult life trying to hear from my godfather, to be honest, and Wicca just kept calling me. It wasn't until I was ready last year to commit

"I am also a Reiki master which is universal life force energy healing. It's a spiritual awakening for me. I always felt like I was meant to do more for the world than be a wife and mother. Not that I don't love it, I do. But I was meant for more, and I'm doing it. And I'm going to continue to strive and succeed. Even if it's within myself. I'm happy."

How has your own family dealt with your father being out yet still being "in the news?"

"My kids are well rounded they aren't effected like we were. They are Contreras anyway, so no one will put it together unless they know me.

"I don't worry too much about that. They're both great kids, they understand the situation with their grandfather, and they both just live their own lives."

Jerry age 13 (1959)

Jerry age 10 (1956)

Jerry with his mother and father 1957

Jerry and Harold (1957)

Jerry's father, grandmother (holding cousin Billy), Uncle Billy, Aunt Barbara, Harold, Jerry

Jerry, Harold (in car) Jerry's mother 1957

Jerry (age 18) on emergency leave from the Marine Corps with Harold

Jerry and second wife, Terry (mother of Jerry's children)

Jerry MCI Walpole 1984

MCI Walpole Family Outing 1984

Jerry, Harold Tillinghast Jr., Harold Old Medium Security Building ACI Rhode Island

Harold Tillinghast and Harold Jr.

Jerry Tillinghast 2018

Chapter 13   *The Evil Men Do*

Enforcer for the Mob

MOB ENFORCER: A thug who uses physical force or the threat of physical force to coerce others.

Jerry Tillinghast is frequently described as a "feared mob enforcer" for the Patriarca Organized Crime family. It is difficult to find an article about him without reading that description. It's become so closely associated with his name that it's difficult to separate the man from the myth.

Jerry has an answer for those who only see him through that prism.

"I didn't work for Ray, I worked for the city of Providence. When the word enforcer is used, they could refer to every parent because if you have certain rules in the house and you break the rules, the parent enforces them."

About reports in the press, Jerry says, "They're always looking to glorify things. It builds up paper sales. It gives the cops more motivation to get our government to pump more money into law enforcement. They say we need more money so we can keep an eye on these people. They got the best racket in the world, police departments do. I don't see how they can allege that I was an enforcer for the mob or anybody else. They've never proved I was an enforcer for anybody. Because I was charged with a couple of cases, most of them dismissed, don't mean what they're saying is true."

Jerry admitted it eats at him. "Yeah, it does. Especially for our families. My family had to deal with that, my kids, my sister, my brothers. People would say 'oh, your Jerry Tillinghast's brother or sister. He's a murderer, he's an enforcer.'"

Jerry's younger sister Sissy, whose name is Helen after her mother, says, "We dealt with it all our lives. We still do that now."

Hanging out at The Bronx Tap, the tough bar in south Providence, linked him to some of the rough crowd usually there. His close affiliation with Gerard Ouimette, himself characterized as a "dangerous mobster," added to Jerry's poor standing with the cops and with the media stories as a "mob enforcer."

Jerry says, "who I hung around with was my choice. If people assume bad things about me because of who I'm with or where I go, that's their problem."

Sometimes, Jerry and his brothers would be bad-mouthed by an individual trying to be a tough guy. While Jerry despises the "enforcer" description, he relishes his reputation for toughness and fearlessness. One particularly unlucky fellow who tried to challenge him paid the price when Jerry spotted him on the street.

"I saw this guy I had been looking for who was talking really bad about my family and me. So, I pulled my car up around the corner and came up in back of him. He was standing in front of a store talking to somebody I grabbed him and spun him around. He said, Jerry what's the matter? I said you been talking all over the city about my brothers and me. We never bothered you. Put your hands up and defend yourself. He tried to sucker punch me, and I hit him with a short right and knocked him out. Blackened both his eyes. Then somebody said he'd call the cops on you, so you'd better get outta here. I told the other guys to get him off the street, and I took off. It was about six blocks from Coffee's (Lounge). I told Coffee to say I'd been there all day."

The police came in, and Coffee backed up Jerry's story. They asked Jerry the same question and when Jerry asked what the problem was one cop told him "You'll find out what the problem is if we find out different."

The enforcer label was pinned on Jerry by police, "because they used to accuse me of shaking down loan sharks and beating people up. They'd see me around the clubs. I got in many, many fights but 95% of the time I'd be sticking up for somebody or if someone was disrespecting a female. I could fight in those days. You grew up in South Providence you had to fight. Plus, I had my brothers who used to bang me around all the time. It's tough for me to talk about it because I don't pride myself on what they call me. I pride myself on being someone who could defend himself.

"The cops charged me with armed robberies and extortion but 95% of the time the cases were dismissed. Anything that happened, if I was in that part of town, I had to be one of the suspects.

"What a waste of taxpayers' money. It's not only me, but it's also a hundred other guys. Leave us the fuck alone. Sometimes I don't know who lives in more of a fantasy world, them or Walt Fuckin' Disney."

He readily admits his choices drew much of the attention from the cops. He reflects on his changing perspective since his days on the street.

"Look, I've lived a lot of what people imagine the life is. But it's not like TV or the movies. That's all bullshit. Popcorn gangsters. I'll tell you what was like in three words, it all sucked. When I realized how it affected my kids and family, if I had to do it over, if I even thought how it would affect my entire family, I would have stayed working and got myself a pension. I still wouldn't have joined the police force, but I probably would have become a fireman because they're my heroes. Them and my mother."

Jerry admits sometimes, he collected money owed to others. "I went out and collected a lot of money for a lot of people. They asked me to do them a favor, I did them a favor, and that was that. Who is collected for and how much, is none of their god-damned business. I told them in nice ways that this is not a good thing. Meaning, owing money. You go to a bank and borrow money, you got to pay it back. There's no difference."

Jerry Tillinghast, Tillie as he was known to many, was a wise guy. A wiseguy's wiseguy according to former Rhode Island State Police Colonel Brendan Doherty.

"I spent half my career working organized crime. A lot of these guys who are supposed to be tough aren't tough. But Jerry is. He's an interesting guy. He has a lot of charisma. A charming guy. The mob needs earners, and they need enforcers. Jerry was both."

As the wiseguy reputation grew, so did the attention Jerry would command from the police. The cases before 1976 built Jerry's renown in the world of the mob. The Bonded Vault case cemented Jerry's reputation as an integral part of the Gerard Ouimette crew and the Patriarca Organized Crime family.

The raucous trial and split verdict, punctuated by Jerry's antics despite the presence of shotgun-toting uniformed Rhode Island State Troopers, remain a Rhode Island legend.

Outside of jail, there were places Jerry liked to go. One of those was the Club Gallery. On any given night, interspersed with the dancers, drinkers, and guys on the hunt for willing women, one could find several members of the mob.

The place was a world unto itself.

Club Gallery

The club started out as a gay bar then morphed into a disco. According to Pat Cortellesa, who worked security, the place was also a favorite of Bobo Marrapese.

"Bobo and his crew would hang there, with them around there was never any trouble. If anybody did get out of line, they were quickly straightened out," Cortellesa said.

"One time, the FBI came in and warned the owner he shouldn't let Bobo hang in the club. The owner was a great stand-up guy. He told the FBI Bobo worked for him as a manager and showed them the books where he kept track of paying Bobo. The feds didn't like it, but there was nothing they could do about it."

Pat confirmed a story Jerry tells about Richard "Moon' Diorio, one of Bobo's guys.

Jerry remembers it well.

"I came in the club one day, and I saw Moonie getting off the elevator with one of the young waitresses. She looked upset, so I asked her what was wrong? She said she didn't want to say anything, but I insisted.

She told me Moonie had forced her to give him a blow job. I said, 'he what?' I called Moonie back over. I asked him what he did, and he just smiled. I knocked him on his ass. The little punk started whining he would tell Bobo. I laughed at him and said, 'go ahead,' Bobo will knock you on your ass as well. You ever touch another girl here and I'll knock you the fuck out permanently.

"I told the girl don't ever get on an elevator with any guy alone. If anybody else bothers you come see me, and it won't ever happen again."

Pat confirmed the whole story. "Jerry and Bobo were like that in the club. They kept things under control."

"Moonie was a punk," Jerry said. "I warned Bobo he'd turned into a rat, but Bobo liked to use him as a gofer. He should've listened to me."

Diorio ended up testifying against Bobo at a later murder trial.

On March 14, 1975, Bobo Marrapese invited Richard 'Dickie' Callei to the Acorn Social Club. Marrapese owned the club and based his operations from there.

Callei, the leader of a rival crew, and Marrapese had a problem. Two of Marrapese's crew killed a member of Callei's crew. Bobo was concerned Callei would retaliate. If someone hit a member of his crew, he would. It would prove to be his undoing in the not too distant future.

At first, Callei enjoyed a cordial welcome in the club. It soon descended into violence. He was stabbed and shot, wrapped in a tarp, and buried in a shallow grave in Rehoboth, Massachusetts. 'Moon' Diorio would later find himself facing a difficult choice. Try to survive on the street as a marked man since Bobo was worried he would talk. Or cooperate with the police, become Bobo's worst nightmare, and disappear into witness protection.

He chose the latter, testifying against Marrapese. Bobo, along with one of his crew, John 'Big John' Chaukoian, were found guilty of Callei's murder.

For the most part, things in the clubs were well-controlled whenever Jerry or his friends were around. The violence contained by the threat of worse violence, out of the view of most.

Outside the clubs, Jerry tried earning money at various legitimate business endeavors.

He often involved his family, and one of these operations

led to an appearance in something other than criminal court. A civil case would pit him against a future Rhode Island Attorney General who happened to be a nun, Arlene Violet.

Violet became the first woman elected in the U.S. to the position of Attorney General earning her the nickname, Atilla the Nun. She set her sights on scam run by Jerry's father and brother.

One of the businesses Jerry started was a paving and landscaping business.

While keeping his job with the city, Jerry would drum up business and send his father with a crew to do the work. On his days off, Jerry ran the crew.

"I was making good money at it, but sometimes my father and brother could be knuckleheads. The whole thing wasn't as bad as it seemed."

Paving the Way to Success

According to former Attorney General Arlene Violet, her first contact with Jerry was a civil case when she worked in the Consumer Protection Division of the AG's office.

Jerry's company was working a scam in the Elmwood section of Providence.

"They would collect maybe a half dozen down payments to asphalt driveways, never did the work and then leave that neighborhood and pick another street. I was head of the Attorney General's Consumer Complaint Division, and we received about twenty complaints."

Violet brought the brothers into court.

"I remember Jerry said, 'Baby, why don't we go for a drink and settle this?'"

The case was dismissed as long as they paid the money back.

Although Jerry denied the incident, particularly the part of asking her out for a drink, Violet is sure it was him. Jerry said it was his brother John and his father who were responsible.

"When I found out what they were doing I made them pay the money back or made sure they did the work. It was just laziness on their part."

Arlene Violet became Rhode Island's Attorney General in 1984 and served one term. She did not have another confrontation with Jerry because he was doing life for the shooting death of George Basmajian.

Violet remembers little trouble on Federal Hill other than bad guys shooting bad guys. She says most of the businesses paid Patriarca for protection. As far as murders that occurred on Federal Hill, Violet says they were easy targets because they were creatures of habit.

"They knew when they stopped to see their mothers for Sunday dinner. Those who were murdered were those who had a habit everybody knew."

Violet kept abreast of mob activities with weekly meetings with Colonel Walter Stone, then Superintendent of the Rhode Island State Police. Although Patriarca was dead by then, the primary concern was who was going to take over for him. The State Police focused a great deal of attention on the mob.

Junior Patriarca, out of respect for the old man, was the obvious choice. He turned out to be largely ineffective.

There were suspicions about Joseph Bevilacqua Sr., Chief Justice of the Rhode Island Supreme Court, having ties to the Patriarca organization.

State Police surveillance followed the Judge to a rendezvous with a woman at a motel in Smithfield. An infamous photograph made its way into the hands of the Providence Journal showing the Chief Justice zipping his fly as he left the motel room.

The State Police wanted the Attorney General to prosecute the judge for adultery, which was still a crime at the time. Prosecutors declined. If they indicted the Judge for such an offense, they argued, they'd have to prosecute half the population of Rhode Island.

Such was the fervor in targeting the mob.

Her office handled some appeals and civil cases brought by Jerry and other inmates about conditions at the prison. But his days of being a force on the street for the mob were behind him.

Jerry did pose a problem within the prison. His wit and intelligence, coupled with his reputation, made him a natural leader. Using the resources of the law library, he filed civil lawsuits about prison conditions and helped other inmates research and file appeals.

He was part of the 'heavies' as they were known who ran the prison as a fiefdom.

Before John Moran became director of the state prison, the evidence pointed to mob guys having the run of the place.

"They would have food brought in, as depicted in the film Goodfellas. There would be prime rib. All true."

In the movie, one of the scenes depicts an inmate cooking steak.

> *Johnny Dio*: How do you like your steak?
> *Paul Cicero*: Medium rare.
> *Johnny Dio*: Huh. An aristocrat.

It was an accurate portrayal of conditions in prison during the 1970s. Inmates living large while serving prison sentences. The inmates made the rules. Gerard Ouimette controlled the operation bringing lobsters, steaks, pasta, and cases of liquor brought into the jail.

During one of these lavish dinners, a photograph depicted a who's who of notorious wise guys enjoying a meal. Gerard and Johnnie Ouimette, Richard Gomes, Ronald Sweet, renowned civil rights lawyer William Kunstler, and George Basmajian.

Violet agrees that's the way it really was until John Moran became director of the Department of Corrections.

"They hated John Moran because he cracked down on all the nonsense."

Chapter 14 *Basmajian Homicide November 1978*

The Winds of November Blow Chilly

November 30, 1978, George Basmajian's last day among the living, began as a cloudy, overcast day in Providence, Rhode Island. Light, early morning fog and rain gave way to clouds and a chilly, forty-two-degree day.

By 9:30 p.m., despite having been followed all day by the State Police and FBI, Basmajian would be dead; nine.38 caliber holes in his body.

Rhode Island State Police Detective Lieutenant Vincent Vespia began his day as part of a surveillance team targeting Basmajian. Vespia wasn't initially scheduled for the surveillance. Another trooper, assigned to the investigation needed time off, so Lt. Vespia volunteered.

Vespia was assisted by fellow Rhode Island State Police Lieutenant Thomas C. Griffin and FBI Special Agents Phil Reilly and Robert Hargraves. The surveillance team took up positions near Basmajian's Johnston, Rhode Island home. During the day the group consisted of as many as six investigators, reduced to three by late afternoon; Vespia, Griffin, and Reilly.

There was little activity during the morning. In the afternoon, the team followed Basmajian and his wife to the Registry of Motor Vehicles. Mrs. Basmajian drove their 1978 Lincoln Continental. Leaving the Registry, George Basmajian now in the driver's seat, the couple drove to Mrs. Basmajian's father's home, also in Johnston.

Later, George Basmajian drove to the Thornton section of Johnston and picked up a friend, David Cianci. The two men then drove to Michael's Lounge at 125 Broadway Providence, arriving between 5:45 and 6:00 p.m. according to Lieutenant Vespia.

Fifteen minutes later, the two left Michael's and drove to a restaurant in Johnston. At 6:45, Basmajian left the restaurant, leaving Cianci, and returned to Michael's Lounge.

At some point, Basmajian and Jerry Tillinghast came outside and spoke on the sidewalk. Vespia noted that Jerry was wearing a golf-type cap and a dark-colored, three-quarter-length jacket with gold lettering on the back. After the conversation, Basmajian left in his Lincoln. Reilly and Griffin followed Basmajian, Vespia remained behind keeping tabs on Michael's Lounge.

At 7:21 p.m., Jerry walked out of the lounge, made a call at a nearby pay phone, then returned to the bar. After a few moments, Jerry came outside and paced the sidewalk. At 8:05 p.m. he crossed the street and walked to a small parking lot next to the Providence Internal Revenue Service. A Cadillac Eldorado arrived, driven by Jerry's brother, Harold Tillinghast.

Both Tillinghast brothers went into Michael's Lounge.

A short time later, George Basmajian returned to Michael's Lounge. Investigators noted he'd changed clothes. Jerry Tillinghast came out and spoke to Basmajian. They briefly returned to Michael's, then drove off in Basmajian's car. Harold Tillinghast was not with them at that time.

Lt. Vespia drove around the block returning to the intersection of Broadway and Dean Street. He spotted Basmajian's car at the light facing west. Vespia turned left on Broadway, and Basmajian ended up right behind him.

At DePasquale Avenue, Basmajian turned right. Vespia lost sight of the vehicle. He turned right at the next intersection, trying to locate Basmajian and Tillinghast.

He didn't find them. Radioing for assistance, the surveillance team headed for likely areas Basmajian might go. First, they went to Johnston. No luck.

Then they headed to the area of St. Rocco's Club, Fourth Ave, Cranston. A place frequented by Gerard Ouimette and his crew.

Lt. Vespia avoided getting too close to the club so as not to be spotted by anyone there. He parked about a half-mile away in the lot of a bowling alley on Elmwood Avenue. Backing his car into a parking spot, he turned off his lights, shut the car off, and waited.

He didn't have to wait long.

A 1974 four-door Mercury color yellow drove past Vespia. Vespia later testified that he could identify all three occupants of the vehicle.

(From the trial transcripts, Lieutenant Vespia on direct examination by Prosecutor Stephen Famiglietti)

Q: Could you tell us who was driving the car?
A: The defendant Gerald Tillinghast
Q: Could you tell us how he was dressed at that time?
A: Wearing a gray-colored cap, golf-type hat, dark-colored jacket. That's all I saw.
Q: And could you tell us who was riding in the front passenger seat?

A: Harold Tillinghast, the defendant

Q: And was he dressed in a similar manner to what you had seen earlier?

A: The only thing I could make out was dark-colored clothing

Q: And could you tell us who, if anybody, was in the back seat?

A: George Basmajian was in the back seat

Q: And were you able to determine at that time what George Basmajian was wearing?

A: I saw him wearing a dark-colored jacket with white sleeves.

The Mercury continued past Vespia and turned onto Elmwood Ave. Vespia notified the rest of the surveillance team, and they followed the car from the bowling alley to Interstate 95 southbound. There were three surveillance cars. Vespia, Lt. Thomas Griffin of the State Police, and Special Agent Phil Reilly of the FBI.

The Mercury took Exit 13, known as the Airport Connector, off the highway. This ramp turns east and crosses over the interstate. As the vehicle negotiated the curve a snow fence, used to prevent snow from blowing onto the highway, blocked the investigators' view of the Mercury for several seconds. When the surveillance team caught up to the Mercury it was stopped at the red light at the intersection of the Airport Connector and Post Road, Warwick.

In the car investigators now saw just two figures.

(From the trial transcripts. Lieutenant Vespia on direct examination by Prosecutor Stephen Famiglietti)

Q: After the car took the airport exit, Exit 13, did you for some period of time lose sight of the car, of the 1974

Mercury?

A: Yes

Q: For approximately how long?

A: A few seconds

Q: Can you explain to the jury why you lost sight of the Mercury?

A: Yes. As I took Exit 13, which veers to the right off 95, it sharply curves to the left, changing direction of travel toward the airport. At that time there was a rather high snow fence. It probably was five or six feet in height. It was erected at that time. That caused the 1974 Mercury to be not clearly in my view as I was negotiating the curve. I was several car lengths behind the Mercury. And because of the existence of the curve in that road, and because of the fact that there was a snow fence on that curve, I lost sight of the Mercury for a very few seconds.

After introducing photographs of the area, Famiglietti continued the direct examination of Lt. Vespia.

Q: At some point in time, did the 1974 Mercury come to a stop somewhere after taking the exit?

A: It did.

Q: Can you tell us where it stopped?

A: It stopped at the red light at the intersection of the Post Road and Airport Connector. That's in the city of Warwick.

Q: And at the time that it stopped, did you also stop?

A: I had to stop for the same red light

Q: And did Agent Reilly also stop?

A: Yes. At that time Agent Reilly's car was in front of my car. He stopped directly behind the '74 Mercury sedan, and I was the third car parked directly behind Agent Reilly's car.

Q: And was there a car parked behind you at the red light?

A: Lt. Griffin in his car pulled up behind me

Q: Do you recall approximately how long that red light stayed red?

A: Several seconds. I (pausing to think) --I didn't time it.

Q: At that point in time, were you able to get a look into the inner portion of the 1974 Mercury?

A: Yes

Q: And what, if anything, did you observe at that time?

A: I observed that there were just two passengers seated in the front seat of the '74 Mercury.

Q: And the person that you had previously seen in the back seat, was he visible?

A: He was not visible at that time

Q: Once you came to that realization, what if anything did you do?

A: Well, we were talking to one another over the radio. And we were concerned that--

(Defense counsel John Cicilline objects to this answer, and the objection is sustained. The court ruled Lt. Vespia could only testify to his own thoughts and actions, not what the other investigators thought.)

The Mercury turned left onto Post Road south then turned right onto Fullerton Street. The investigators decided to back off since that area was industrial and they were concerned the men in the car would spot them and that Basmajian had been dropped off somewhere. They stayed in the area and waited.

Q: Did you happen to look at your watch at the time that you were stopped at that red light at the intersection of the Post Road exit?

A: Yes

Q: And approximately what time was it at that time?

A: Approximately 9:15

Q: And when the vehicle, the 1974 Mercury, took a left at the Post Road, would you tell us what it next did?

A: It took the next intersection, it negotiated a right turn. The name of the street was Fullerton Street.

Q: As the vehicle took a left onto Post Road from the red light, were you able to get a look at the operator of the vehicle again?

A: Yes

Q: And at that point in time, were you able to identify who the operator of the vehicle was again?

A: Yes

Q: And who was that?

A: (Pointing) Gerald Tillinghast, the defendant

Q: When the vehicle took a right onto Fullerton Street, did you follow it?

A: I did not

Q: Did any of the other members of the surveillance team follow it?

A: We did not

Q: Could you tell us why not?

A: The purpose of the surveillance was to surveil George Basmajian, bearing in mind that he may be involved in criminal activity. In light of the fact that at that intersection we'd only saw two individuals in that car--

(Defense attorney Cicilline again objected to Vespia's use of the word 'we.' The court cautioned Lieutenant Vespia to only testify about his own observations, and the trial continued with Lieutenant Vespia answering the question again.)

A: In order to continue the surveillance down Fullerton Street, I felt that we most certainly would be identified as police officers. It's an industrial area, not heavily traveled that time of the night. My plan was to give the occupants of that car time to do whatever we suspected them of doing down in that area. I thought we had missed something--

(Again, Cicilline objected to the use of the word 'we.' After a sidebar discussion the Judge overruled the objection saying the language was a common and understandable explanation for the Lieutenant's actions.)

A: (Continuing) By virtue of the fact I didn't see Basmajian at that time in the back seat, I thought he may have gotten out of the car and I didn't see it. I didn't know what was happening at that time. I didn't know what we had. To take them down Fullerton Street, positively, in my opinion, we would have been made.

(The court reporter asked for clarification of the term 'made.')

A: We would have been identified. That's the police term for identified. We would have been identified as police officers. For that reason, a decision was made via radio between the three of us, don't take him down Fullerton Street, let them go down there, give them time to do whatever they went there for. That was our plan. That was the plan we followed.

Q: Now, what did you do at that point in time?

A: We waited a short period of time, approximately five minutes, and then Lt. Griffin, Agt. Reilly, and myself infiltrated the industrial-type complex which is west of Post Road, near the area which we last observed the '74 Mercury containing the two defendants traveling.

Q: And do you recall, was the 1974 Mercury located by one of the members of the surveillance team?

A: Yes

Q: And do you know who located it?

A: Yes

Q: Who was that?

A: Agt. Reilly of the FBI.

Q: How did you come to that knowledge?

A: At 9:20 p.m. I received a radio call from Agt. Reilly. As a result of what I learned from that radio call, I met Agt. Reilly behind--

Q: Where did you--

A: --behind the National Car Rental Service, which is located at the intersection of Fresno Road and Post Road.

Q: And what did you do when you arrived at the location at Fresno Road?

A: I met Agt. Reilly at that location. We both approached the '74 Mercury together

(After several questions about the lighting, general area,

194

and the partially obscured dealer plate Vespia had seen on the car now missing, Famiglietti continued)

Q: Did you look inside the vehicle at that point in time?
A: I did
Q: Tell us what you observed?
A: George Basmajian dead in the back seat.
Q: Aside from the fact that he was dead, what specifically did you observe about his body?
A: What appeared to be a huge head wound, gushing blood
Q: Did you open the door?
A: No
Q: Did Agt. Reilly open the door?
A: No
Q: Did Lt. Griffin arrive on the scene?
A: By that time, he was there, yes.

<u>(At this point a recess was called in the trial)</u>

After finding Basmajian dead, Vespia and Reilly went to look for the Tillinghasts. Lt. Griffin stayed at the crime scene.

An intriguing aspect came to light during Griffin's testimony after the discovery of Basmajian's body. Lieutenant Griffin testified to putting out a broadcast for Jerry Tillinghast then, after further radio contact with the other investigators, added a broadcast for Harold.

Why the original transmission was only for Jerry Tillinghast was never explained. Nor did anyone explain why the radio alert was limited to State Police and not all police departments in the area.

Vespia and Reilly went to St. Rocco's first. Not finding the brothers there, they went to Michael's Lounge. They saw Jerry and Harold sitting at a table with Attorney Paul Dimaio and others.

Vespia placed Jerry up against a wall, handcuffed him, and took him out.

Jerry was still wearing the same jacket. Vespia testified he noticed blood on the sleeve. Other witnesses testified the club was dark and the blood a small amount. The blood later tested to be the same type as Basmajian's, and Jerry's.

There is a conflict as to how and when Harold was placed under arrest. Agent Reilly testified he placed Harold in custody after Jerry was handcuffed.

Witnesses say Vespia and Reilly took Jerry out to the state police cruiser and Harold was left inside with Paul Dimaio. Paul walked outside to speak with the officers, and Harold stuck his head out the door yelling at the cops, "Where are you taking my brother?"

It was at the point, witnesses say, Harold was arrested. All the witnesses agree that Vespia and Reilly focused on Jerry before turning their attention to Harold.

Reilly testified he didn't search Harold at the time he placed him under arrest because "it didn't occur to me."

There is another curious aspect of Reilly's testimony. When asked if he could identify the individuals in the stolen car while they followed it to Warwick, Reilly was sure about Jerry and Basmajian. Yet testified he only caught a brief glimpse of Harold in profile and could not describe his clothing.

In the confusion and adrenaline driven moment, these conflicting accounts are difficult to reconcile. It's also intriguing that the State Police never notified other agencies to look for the Tillinghast brothers.

From the moment they discovered the body it took some time for them to drive first to St. Rocco's and then Michael's lounge. St. Rocco's was three miles away and another five miles from there to Michael's

The Providence police station was less than half a mile from Michael's. Providence would have uniform officers and detectives on the street able to be there within seconds.

Same with St. Rocco's? Cranston PD could have officers there within moments of being notified.

Why not send Providence officers to Michael's and Cranston officers to St. Rocco's?

Why not a statewide alert to every agency to be on the lookout for the Tillinghast brothers?

Why introduce a delay in locating the brothers?

The answers are elusive. Yet Paul Dimaio is sure of one thing.

"I walked in Michael's at about 8:35 p.m. and Harold was there. No way he could have killed that man."

For the last six hours of his life, George Basmajian had a team of investigators following his every move. And yet, despite all that surveillance, through the momentary obstruction of the surveillance team's view, Basmajian was dead, and the Tillinghasts were under arrest, facing life in prison.

Chapter 15 *Trial*

Wednesday, July 11, 1979, after completing jury selection, the trial of the State of Rhode Island vs. Gerald and Harold Tillinghast began before Justice Antonio Almeida.

In a classic Rhode Island twist, the Judge himself would later be convicted of accepting bribes in civil cases from a local Rhode Island lawyer, finding himself in the very prison to which he had sentenced many defendants, including Jerry and Harold.

In his opening statements, Prosecutor Stephen Famiglietti, who would later go on to successfully prosecute Claus von Bulow for attempted murder, said the state would show beyond any reasonable doubt that the defendants murdered George Basmajian.

In a criminal trial, the opening remarks by the prosecution are not evidence. It is supposed to be an opportunity for the state to lay out a map of its case for the jury to follow. But, as in any complicated matter, often the words of the Prosecutor carry great weight with the jury.

This was to be a trial of credibility pitting the reputation of the Rhode Island State Police and the Federal Bureau of Investigation against the words of two men closely associated with organized crime and their alibi witnesses.

In such cases, the scientific evidence and expert testimony

often cloud the jury's perspective more than assists them in reaching a decision. It would be witness credibility that would be the deciding factor in this case.

The prosecution knew it and, more critically, the defense knew it.

Juries are always the wild card in these proceedings. Some are diligent in listening to the Judge's instructions, rulings, and admonitions. Some ignore them out of preconceived notions or experiences. In the final analysis, once the jury enters deliberations, anything is possible.

Since the time of this trial, jury selection has become more science than art. Where once defense attorneys and prosecutors relied on their experience to select or exclude jurors, now psychological profiles and personality analysis is used. But in 1979, lawyers relied on the old school method to get a jury most favorable to their case.

In this trial, there are some crucial elements which rose to the surface during witness testimony. The explanation for the position of the shooter(s), their distance to the victim, and the sequence of events suggests several possibilities.

Dr. William Sturner (the long-time Rhode Island State Medical Examiner) testified the head wounds, showing fouling and stippling, were consistent with someone firing within a maximum of three feet and is more consistent with shooting within 6 inches.

Fouling is burned gunpowder residue. Stippling, sometimes called tattooing, is unburned gunpowder and debris particles causing puncture abrasions. They both indicate close proximity of the gun barrel to the victim.

Dr. Sturner, testifying as an expert, indicated the first three rounds were fired a close range into the torso, with two of the shots likely to be fatal. The head wounds were also fired at close range while the victim lay on his left side on the back seat of the car.

State Police crime photos show Basmajian's lying in this position with his head behind the driver's seat.

Under cross-examination by the defense, Dr. Sturner testified that it would be "highly unlikely" a right-handed driver could fire into the torso of the back seat passenger while negotiating a curve off the highway.

The ballistics examination said the six.38 caliber bullets recovered from the head and three.38 caliber bullet recovered from the torso were fired from the same weapon. Recall the testimony that Jerry Tillinghast was driving when Basmajian disappeared from view. Based on this scenario, Jerry would have to fire the gun three times while driving, reload at some point, and fire six more rounds into Basmajian's head.

If the initial rounds were fired while the car drove around the curve on the off-ramp, then the others were most likely fired after they had parked the car.

Someone had to reload the weapon, fire six more rounds at point blank range, and leave the area in the five or so minutes the police remained away from the area.

It would lend credence to the shooter being the passenger, not Jerry while driving the car.

The weapon was never recovered. Tests done on Jerry and Harold were inclusive in determining whether or not they had fired a gun.

Prosecution experts testified to the blood found in four separate locations on Jerry's jacket. The tests on three of the blood splatter areas could only determine it was human blood. In one area, the blood type was identified as type "O."

Due to insufficient quantities of blood, they were unable to further determine the Rh factor or other identifying characteristics.

Both Basmajian and Jerry had "O" type blood. Harold Tillinghast had type "A." "O" type blood is the most common human blood type carried by 45% of the human population.

Defense experts, relying on the same evidence, offered a different scenario. Dr. Henry Lee, the head of the Connecticut State Police Laboratory, who would go on to testify in the O.J. Simpson case, offered a different opinion on the blood found on Jerry's jacket sleeve.

Dr. Lee believed the blood was consistent with droplets from a nosebleed, not blood splatter from a gunshot wound. The amount recovered from the jacket, Lee testified, was consistent with this explanation.

The defense put a doctor on the stand who testified he was treating Jerry for a severe case of nose-bleeds. He corroborated Dr. Lee's testimony the blood was consistent with such a condition.

Like in most cases, the effect of expert testimony is never known with any certainty. Often the scientific jargon clouds the purpose. In this case, the impact of the expert testimony about the blood and hairs on the jury's verdict will never be known.

After the lengthy trial, the jury deliberated just a few days. They returned a verdict of guilty for Jerry and Harold. Judge Almeida denied defense motions for a new trial and sentenced both men to life in prison.

Paul Dimaio was adamant about Harold's innocence. He never asked Jerry about the case, he didn't need to. His only purpose was to right what he perceived as a grievous miscarriage of justice.

He would appear at every parole hearing for Harold and make the same contention. He stands by the position to this day.

But once a jury reaches a guilty verdict, the only recourse is through the appellate process. No matter the efforts made to secure a new trial, the court upheld the verdict.

Harold did his time and eventually made parole, dying within just a few short years of his release. He was 61 years old.

Chapter 16 *Prison Years*

Life Inside

Despite the bitterness following his conviction and sentence for the Basmajian murder, Jerry eventually settled in at the ACI. It took at least five years for him to accept that his life would never be the same after the judge handed him a life sentence.

It would be his brother's fate, linked to a code Jerry soon realized was a myth, that troubled him most.

Known as part of a group called "the heavies," Jerry got along with most corrections officers, especially after he was given the job of porter for his cell block. One corrections officer, who quit the job in disgust after 10 years in maximum security, called it a world of its own.

"It's not like being a police officer where you deal with a guy for a few hours. You deal with these guys on a day to day basis. Some guys doing life could be with you for your whole career. Relationships evolve. Some guys are pieces of shit and others you get to know as part of a community."

He remembered Jerry well.

"Like other guys of his caliber, he wasn't looking for trouble. They kind of police themselves. In the 70's they had morals as opposed to gangs like today. We didn't have rapists and child molesters in the general population. They got segregated immediately. Jerry and his associates wouldn't be around those people in prison just like they wouldn't be around them on the street. But as time evolved that changed."

On example of jobs Jerry had in prison was in New Hampshire. An opening became available, and Jerry made friends with the librarian named Cathy who he described as tough but fair, "and didn't take no crap."

Cathy told Jerry he could work the copy machine if he didn't make her fire him. "Don't get like everybody else and screw up, so I have to fire you."

It didn't take Jerry long before he worked his way into the computer lab where he stayed for two years. Good jobs in the state prison system are scarce. Jobs themselves are hard to find.

"Say there were 700 people in maximum and there are only two hundred jobs," Jerry explained. "That means there are 500 inmates with nothing to do and sooner or later with idle time on their hands, the thought process becomes very creative for entertainment. Most of us were all friends so if the administration tried to fuck one, we're going to band together and say fuck you! In their minds, if they have inadequate feelings, that's not our fucking problem. As long as we're not doing anything to promote problems. A lot are intimidated because of who we were.

"I followed all the rules and regulations, even the stupid ones because those are the ones that get you jammed up. When I go a long time without getting written up they think, he's just sliding, just manipulating the system. Manipulating my fucking ass, I'm doing it because I just want to stay out of trouble so I can move through the system. They can stick their theories up their ass."

Someone at the ACI who knew Jerry Tillinghast and served as a high-ranking official in the system, but wished to remain anonymous, had remarkable observations about him.

"This guy is not a liar; this guy was something. When I was in college, I remember State Police Lieutenant Mike Urso speaking about him. Jerry held a hell of a lot of status in the New England mob.

"Gerard Ouimette's book made you think he (Ouimette) was

second-in-command. That's not true. It's a lot of crap."

This officer served as a deputy warden and was a corrections officer for 36 years. This is how he recalls his interaction with Jerry and his brother Harold.

"I started working there in '78. Jerry had come in on that Basmajian thing. They picked him up and his brother at Michael's Lounge. That's when he came into the prison system...him and his brother, Harold. I was assigned to maximum security. He spent two years with us until he got shipped out of state.

"Jerry was a force to be reckoned. He was one of two terrifying guys. One being Frank 'Bobo' Marrapese and the other, Jerry Tillinghast.

"There was a professional line between us in the years I worked with Jerry. Jerry is a very likable guy. You must understand he is capable of doing what he has done. He was very much involved in the New England mob scene. They owned the Club Martinique, one of the best twin lobster specials in Rhode Island.

"Jerry was a rough and tumble guy but a sharp dresser with a long trench coat. The women loved him. He was liked among a circle of people who knew him."

Asked why he thought Jerry turned out the way he did, the former guard had this observation.

"This is my theory, and I spoke to him like I'm speaking to you, I blame it on his bad discharge out of the Marine Corps. Jerry did his time in Vietnam. I believe he finished his 13 months in Vietnam. He DD'ed (dishonorable discharged) out.

"I asked him why he went the way he did. He could have been the Colonel of the State Police if he went that route. He is sharp. He's an organizer. He's nobody's fucking fool. He was dangerous in the prison system. They didn't want to keep him around long and shipped him out of state. If anyone could have gathered a crew together, it was him. He had that ability, but I believe it all started with the Marine Corps. I think Jerry would have intervened in the rape of that Vietnamese woman.

"When he went that way into a life of crime, he threw himself right into it. There were no other options available to him. He didn't go to college. He wasn't going to be a fucking lawyer.

"When Jerry was stabbed in the back of his neck with a broken license plate, I was on duty.

"He was stabbed in the fucking neck twice. All the guy did was piss him off. I took him and his brother Harold to a rear hall. It was a vendetta, a payback. Somebody's daughter talked somebody into it. They blamed Jerry for their father's death.

"Jerry is a smart, smart guy, well read and an organizer. A guy like that can do a lot of fucking damage. Lt. Mike Urso told us Jerry's status was much the same as a made guy. He and his crew were money makers. Jerry's strength is a straight-up guy. That's what makes him dangerous because he's not playing. He was a straight-up guy."

Jerry's time in prison was not without its comic moments. While he and Harold were segregated from the outside world, they were still aware of national and international events.

Reflecting both a sense of duty and a fundamental misunderstanding of international relations, Harold came up with an idea along the lines of the movie *The Dirty Dozen*. Harold wanted to interject himself and select fellow inmates onto the international stage.

Hostage Rescue

In November 1979, Iranian students attacked the U.S.

Embassy in Iran and took dozens of hostages. Although some were released quickly, 52 U.S. citizens were held for 444 days finally being released a day after Ronald Reagan was sworn in as President of the United States.

During the entire 444 days, President Jimmy Carter failed to negotiate the release of the hostages. That is when Harold Tillinghast took pen in hand and volunteered a group of inmates to go to Iran and rescue them.

There were obvious problems with Harold's letter. First, he wrote it and told none of his fellow inmates he was offering them to President Carter. The list was a formidable one under the heading of Freedom Force One. They included Frank 'Bobo' Marrapese, Thomas Firth, Andrew Merola, Michael Correro, Nick Pari, Paul Garzaro, and Robert Holmstead. That list also included Harold and Jerry.

Jerry recalled finding out about the letter.

"I said, 'Harold, what the fuck were you thinking? He didn't even ask anybody."

In the letter, Harold picked specific functions they would perform during the rescue.

One guy would be in charge of transportation because he was in for stealing cars. Another would be a sniper because he was a good shot. He told the President he wasn't looking for early release, he just wanted to volunteer to help out the country.

Harold received a reply from one of Carter's secretaries, thanking him for offering his services.

"I'll tell you one thing," Jerry said. "If we were ever approved, I would have gone in a heartbeat. Regardless of what I did or didn't do, I'm still a patriot. If someone hurts our country, fuck 'em, I'll kill 'em. Forget negotiating."

During the crisis in Iran, three Iranian drug dealers were

brought to the prison. They were placed in a holding cell in the area where Jerry was performing porter duties. His brother Harold was also on the work crew.

Jerry, once a Marine always a Marine, wasted no time in greeting the latest guests of the prison. Guests he perceived as enemies of the United States. He and some other inmates blocked the three from leaving their cell for anything, including food.

"I entered their cell and slapped the shit out of them."

The Iranians maintained they didn't support Ayatollah Khomeini calling him "a piece of shit."

Using the handle of a broom, Jerry and some of the other ACI inmates created a banner which read "When you free our hostages we'll free your hostages."

Inmates continued to block the cell door, keeping the inmates locked inside. It soon drew the attention of the corrections officers. One captain asked Jerry to let the Iranians go so they could eat, but he refused. Some guards were laughing and appeared to enjoy the ACI version of the hostage crisis.

The situation ended when Jerry and the other inmates had to return to their cells. The guards moved the Iranians to another section of the prison.

The prison administration was getting nervous at what could have been a dangerous riot situation.

"Shit like that can happen. It's a whole different world in there," Jerry reflected. "I bet they moved the Iranians to another place in the system and put them under protective custody."

Jerry was sent to New Hampshire State Prison in 1994 after being again kicked out of the ACI. While waiting for further processing, he noticed Spanish guys isolating certain people they could intimidate.

One morning, going through the line where everyone had to

squeeze through a gate to go to chow, two Spanish guys left their group and moved up in line, leaving an opportunity for Jerry. He stepped in front of the men.

Suddenly, he was shoved from behind. Turning, he saw the pair glaring at him. One said, "Hey, you cut the line."

Jerry described what happened next,

"Don't you ever put your hands on me again you motherfucker. The guy says we'll talk again, I said where I come from we'll talk now, and punched both of them in the mouth."

The guards on duty saw the incident, and Jerry found himself in segregation.

"The people who saw it were dumbfounded because they never saw anybody do that especially go against other cliques by yourself."

One of the Spanish inmates Jerry had beaten up was brought into segregation at the same time. Jerry told a porter, the guy who cleaned the cells when the inmates were out during a recreation period, to tell the Spanish guy to come to the recreation area so they could finish things.

"The porter told me the guy said he was all set, he don't want no more."

Jerry and the Spanish guy straightened things out and eventually became friends.

"After 30 days I went back to the original area, but everyone was avoiding me. I went over to the black guys and asked what was going on."

Jerry was older than most of the others, and from out of town, so they assumed he was there for a reason, maybe a stool pigeon or for protection. The black group said he could hang with them, but Jerry explained that he wanted no one to put their hands on him.

Things were calm, and the inmates, including Jerry, were soon out in the general population looking for the best place to work. Within a month he was working in the kitchen. He had access to plenty of food until he suffered an elbow injury making kitchen duty very difficult.

Jerry's fellow inmate friend named Steve from Rhode Island worked in the education and law library.

"That's one of the reasons they wanted him out of Rhode Island because he was helping ACI inmates sue the state. Jerry was a smart guy and always willing to help other inmates."

There are a couple of things you don't want to be in prison. Rapists and child molesters don't fare well with other prisoners, many of whom have wives, girlfriends, and kids.

But for those other inmates, some things can get you in deep trouble with other prisoners. Jerry says there is no lower form of life in the general population than a thief.

"The worst thing in the prison world is a room thief."

This is how Jerry explains it: "You work hard for the stuff you can get at the canteen. You get your money for cosmetics, and that's all you got, a fucking piece of shit tries to steal it, and they think they can get away with it because they don't want to do anything. Nothing worse than a room thief. You better set them straight about it right from the beginning or they'll rob you blind.

"You gotta take care of yourself and your stuff. Nobody's gonna do it for you. Survival is a daily event.

"You walk out of your cell door, you never know what you're walking into. For long-term survival, only the strong survive. There are predators, and if you let them push you around and don't stand up for yourself, one thing leads to another and people try to make a victim out of you.

"You learn tactics survival. Just like in the Marine Corps, you learn from the veterans, the guys who've been there. One of the tricks was to get ahold of phone books and string them together. You'd wear it under your clothes like a vest.

"If anyone tries to shank you, the books protect your body. People think some prisons are comfortable living, They ain't. Every prison is a jungle of predators and prey. You better learn to protect yourself, or you won't survive."

Earning a Prison Reputation

Prison officials knew Jerry could be bad news.

"I could start a riot with the snap of a finger. There were quite a few people who could do the same thing. Systematically, they were getting rid of the guys they couldn't control. We had a lawsuit against the administration about the ventilation, the smoking. I got asthma, so we sued them.

"I figured if I went to Florida, got transferred, I'd call my relatives and have a better chance of getting parole. I said if they send me out right away, I'd drop the lawsuit. I tried to use it as a bargaining chip.

"The prison administration ignored me.

"They wanted me out of there, but I didn't have much chance of making parole. They blamed me for all the unrest and problems.

"Every time something happened, they figured I was behind it. I would be in my fucking cell minding my own business."

Jerry remained at the ACI until being transferred to Walpole state prison in Massachusetts from 1980 until 1985 because of his trouble with prison director John Moran.

It was in Walpole where Jerry met another legendary member of the Patriarca family, Enrico 'Henry' Tameleo.

211

Tameleo was known as 'the referee' for his ability to negotiate problems between various factions. He was serving a life sentence for the 1966 murder of Edward 'Teddy' Deegan. The conviction was largely based on the testimony of Joe 'the Animal' Barbosa, a mob killer turned cooperating witness. The FBI also received information from Steven 'Rifleman' Flemmi, then a confidential informant, identifying Tameleo, Peter Limone, Louis Greco, and Joseph Salvati.

In 2000, a special prosecutor investigating the FBI's use of informants in the Whitey Bulger matter determined that Barbosa and Flemmi were responsible for the murders and the FBI was aware of the false information used to convict the men.

While Jerry was in Walpole, he would take care of Henry who was in poor health.

"There were these guys that Henry let have access to his account. They were supposed to buy stuff for Henry, things like a daily newspaper.

"I found out they were spending Henry's money on themselves, so I confronted them. I told them if they kept taking Henry's money, it would be the last thing they ever did.

"When I told Henry, he said not to worry about it. It was not a big deal. I didn't like them doing that because he was a nice old guy, a man of honor, and deserved respect.

"I'd sit with him and listen to him talk about things. I liked Henry, he treated me well."

In 1985, Jerry was kicked out of Walpole because officials thought he was planning a race riot.

"I hit a Muslim in the head with a hammer."

Henry Tameleo died the same year Jerry returned to the ACI. But the case that put him in prison for life would collapse from the fallout of the FBI/Whitey Bulger scandal.

From the National Registry of Exonerations,

"In the summer and fall of 2000, a special prosecutor investigating the FBI's use of informants came across numerous documents from 1965 demonstrating that agents knew Barboza and Flemmi had committed the murder without the involvement of Greco, Limone, Tameleo or Salvati – including reports made directly to FBI Director J. Edgar Hoover. In December of 2000, a Massachusetts Superior Court judge held a hearing to consider releasing Limone based on information in these memos, and on January 5, 2001, Limone was released. All charges against Limone and Salvati were dismissed on January 31, 2001.

In 2003, the Massachusetts House Committee on Government Reform condemned the FBI for failing to turn over documents that would have exonerated Limone. The District Attorney's Office that originally prosecuted the case posthumously dismissed charges against Louis Greco in 2004 and against Henry Tameleo in 2007. U.S. District Judge Nancy Gertner ordered the federal government to pay a total of $102 million. Salvati was awarded $29 million, Limone was awarded $26 million, and $47 million was awarded to the estates of Greco and Tameleo. This award was affirmed by the United States Court of Appeals for the First Circuit in 2009. In 2012, the Department of Justice dropped its appeal of nearly $1 million in costs and fees awarded to the lawyers who brought the lawsuit[21]."

Back at the ACI, Jerry sticking up for a friend cost him another infraction.

"It was just jailhouse fucking bullshit. But the administration

---

21

https://www.law.umich.edu/special/exoneration/Pages/casedetail.aspx?caseid=3674

hated me for it. They wanted to screw a guy over something he didn't start. I wasn't gonna let that happen. If it cost me a missed chance at parole that's just the way it was."

The bullshit then took a turn for the more serious.

Shortly after his return from Walpole, Jerry was stabbed by a fellow inmate named, Allen Brash. No criminal charges were brought because Jerry refused to give a statement.

Brash stabbed Jerry in the neck with a jagged piece of a license plate. The story of how and why it happened indicates how fragile life can be when people are living in a closed environment for extended periods.

"An individual came up to me and said another individual called him a stool pigeon. I asked him if he was a stool pigeon. He said no. I told him he should have punched the guy in the mouth. I told him to defend himself. I told him he couldn't be in jail and have people going around saying he was a rat. He said he wanted to get even with the kid and I said I didn't give a fuck. I don't care if you kill each other.

A day or two later I'm in the maximum-security print shop where I worked. This same guy comes by and says hi Jerry how you doing? He said something else, but I don't have a problem with him, so I'm not paying attention. Inconspicuously, he goes and comes back with a piece of a license plate. It was all cut up, a good solid piece. Now I'm bending over counting some envelopes to be shipped out, and I get this smack on the back of my neck. Well, I thought someone was fucking around with me and punched me in the neck. So, I jumped up, and it was him, and he jumped back because I guess he thought I was gonna fall down, ya know?"

Jerry had been stabbed with a piece of a license plate shaped into a knife.

"I jumped up and said, why you motherfucker. I used to run

the machine to cut paper, and I came around right into him. I had to get the knife off him, and he got me a couple more times, but I got him. I knocked him out, and he wasn't getting up.

"We had a dark room where you develop film and a friend of mine came out of it and he had this mop handle with the metal end on it, and when I turned to the guy who stabbed me he was gone. See, when I hit him and sent him down his head struck the end of a fuckin table. I was gonna jump on him, but I might have landed on the blade, so I didn't. I was then gonna get something and drive it into his throat, but by then he was gone. A cop friend of his got him up, and he was gone."

Jerry thought the kid saw him and another man talking and thought they were planning to give the ok to pipe to him.

"The kid was high. One thing I give him credit for was having the balls to make a move on me. If he wasn't high, he would never have got out of there. Because when you're high, all your senses are more alert. He can be thankful he was high that day."

Following the stabbing, the maximum-security section of the prison went into immediate lockdown. The lockdown was lifted a day later after ACI officials talked to a supervisor the inmates respected.

Prison officials, concerned about Jerry exacting his own form of justice, transferred Brash to Florida.

After he recovered, Jerry again requested a transfer to Florida. He says it had nothing to do with Brash, prison officials felt differently.

The transfer request was denied.

In 1988, he and brother Harold were sent to minimum security where they were awarded work release. It went well for about six months until Jerry's young daughter visited the work site. He spent the next 20 years in medium security.

"That's a hell of an infraction."

In 1990, Jerry's request for transfer to Florida came through. Circumstances had changed. The administration was less concerned over Jerry trying to get at the man who stabbed him than eliminating the problems Jerry caused them by being in the ACI.

The change of heart by the state was part of a deal for Jerry dropping a suit about prison conditions. Jerry's complaint about the ventilation system causing asthma might bring more prisoners into the lawsuit.

The state would agree to his transfer in exchange for Jerry dropping the suit.

"I didn't give a shit about Brash. He was high when he went after me. Just more prison bullshit. I wanted to get to Florida because I thought I'd have a better shot at parole. I had family there. Somewhere I could be paroled to. Away from Rhode Island, I was out of sight, out of mind. There was no way the Rhode Island Parole board was gonna let me out."

While he was in Florida, he received word that his father had died. He was brought back for the funeral a week late, which infuriated him.

Jerry's third wife was Gloria. He met when she was in her early 20's and working at a club in downtown Providence. Gloria knew about him and his reputation.

"I made it a point to meet him," she remembered.

She also recalled a time when they were walking together near Michael's Lounge when he spotted a police car, apparently keeping an eye on him, and dropped his pants.

"I was humiliated."

216

Nevertheless, she and Jerry married in 1992 when he was in Florida. They never had children.

Father Figure to Others

Rob Rinn knew Jerry and Harold Tillinghast when he was growing up. He hung around with Jarrod, Jerry's youngest son.

When he turned sixteen, he found himself out on his own. His father had left the family, leaving his mother to find a way to survive on her own.

Rob started looking for ways to make money. He'd noticed some older kids making money shining shoes, so he took a pillowcase, some old rags, some black and brown polish one of the other kids gave him and set out on his own.

Making his way around the clubs in Providence, he narrowed his stops down to the most profitable. Places where guys had money and were willing to throw it around.

One of those clubs was owned by Bobo Marrapese. One day inside Bobo's place, Robb was busy earning money. Bobo approached him and asked him why he carried his stuff in a pillowcase.

"Why don't you have a shine box?

"Can't afford one," Rob answered.

"Hang on, kid," Bobo replied. A short time later, Bobo returned with a shine box and gave it to him.

"It made it easier for me to make money and help out my mother," Robb said. "I looked up to those guys."

As is often the case with young men with little restrictions, Robb eventually crossed the line into stealing cars and ripping off drug dealers.

He emulated the tough guys, never shied away from fights, and began building his own street reputation. One confrontation almost cost him his life when he took on a guy who pulled a knife and sliced Robb open, giving him a nasty scar across much of his stomach and chest. He came close to dying.

One of these adventures landed him back in prison. Rinn settled in to do his time.

Until Jerry and Harold found him. Harold arranged for him to be moved to a two-person cell.

"Do you know how to cook turkeys?" Harold asked.

"Yeah, why?" Rinn answered.

"Good, meet me in the kitchen tomorrow."

The next morning Rinn walked to the kitchen and Harold pointed to a bunch of turkeys.

"Stuff 'em and cook 'em and I'll tell you where to deliver them when they're done."

Rinn finished cooking the turkeys and Harold gave him a list of cells for him to deliver the dinners. On the way, a guard stopped him.

"What you got there?"

"Turkey. Want some?"

"Sure," the guard smiled.

Rinn said Harold always put extras in for the guards.

A short while later, Rinn and his cellmate were sleeping in their cell. The door opened and in walked Jerry Tillinghast.

Rinn recounted the story.

"Jerry comes in and looks at my cellmate. 'Pack your shit, your movin,'

'Why?' the guy asked.

'Because I said so, now pack your shit or I will.'

"The guy was gone, and Jerry moved in. He'd decided to keep an eye on me.

"There were rules with Jerry. He didn't smoke. He didn't allow smoking anywhere near him.

"One day, I was sneaking a cigarette in the back of the cell when Jerry walked in. He found the cigarettes and crushed them. Then, he made me go stand in the corner. Made me stay there until he said I could move.

"It became a running joke with us. Anytime I'd do something Jerry didn't like, he'd send me to the corner. I still joke with him to this day about it.

"Another time I was sitting on my bunk and Jerry was on his. He said, 'Hey, come down here.'

"I jumped down, and Jerry pointed at my pile of stuff and then at his shelf.

'Notice anything?' he asked.

"His shelf was perfectly neat. Everything was organized by size, all in straight lines. Even the labels all faced the same direction.

"My pile was just tossed in a heap.

'Yeah, you're neat and organized,' I said.

'Exactly, and that way if anything goes missing you'll know right away. Do yourself a favor and learn something here.'

"A few weeks later, the guy who stabbed me ended up in jail with us. I hadn't given the guy up to the cops, I didn't work that way. I wanted to deal with this myself.

"Jerry figured out who the guy was, and pulled me aside.

'Listen, you got a family, right? You want to go home to them, don't you? You make a move on that guy, and you'll never get out of here. Listen to me. Outside, his time will come. In here you steer clear, understand?'

"I learned a lot from Jerry and Harold. They kept me out of trouble in the can and paid attention even after I got out. I have nothing but respect for them. They were smart, and they took good care of me even though I wasn't family.

"They cared about me. Jerry and Harold were like uncles to me. It says something about them as people."

Jerry's concern for his fellow inmates affected other areas of life inside. Besides helping with appeals and case research, Jerry found ways to enrich the environment with creative activities.

Anything that helped pass the time, and reduced opportunity for trouble, was a good thing.

Reading Providence in Prison

Jerry and a group of inmates formed a reading group. A Brown University History Professor, Paul Buhle, with interest in pathways to criminal behavior, was invited to meet with the group.

The discussion, sponsored by Reading Rhode Island, was run by the Department of State Library Services. A grant from the Rhode Island Committee for the Humanities devoted to books about or by Rhode Islanders funded the program.

The topic was the book *Providence by Geoffrey Wolff*[22]. *Providence* is a work of fiction. But its cast of characters is not dissimilar to the real world of Providence with its organized crime, corrupt politicians, street denizens, and hard-boiled cops.

On February 3, 1987, The Providence Journal did a featured story by G. Wayne Miller about the group and the discussions with Professor Buhle.

Jerry is quoted extensively in the article. He'd taken exception to the way the book characterized Providence and the State of Rhode Island.

"Hey, I'm in jail," Jerry is quoted. "I broke the law, whatever you want to call it. But I'm still proud of my state. They make it sound as if the price is there, that whatever you want you can buy. Whatever side of society I got caught up in, I can't see it as a corrupt state. It's mostly honest, hard-working people—it's an insult to them."

Professor Buhle, even after all this time, recalled the meeting.

---

[22] Providence by Geoffrey Wolff ISBN 978-0679732778

"Jerry was clearly the intellectual of the group, by a long shot, and greatly admired because... he was the only one who planned his crimes."

During the discussion, Jerry said, "There are certain things in this book that me and other individuals in this room can relate to people out there. Wolff definitely had real people in mind."

Professor Buhle said he tried to get incoming freshmen students at Brown to think about the routes of involvement people like Jerry Tillinghast followed.

"In my introduction, I used to suggest the interlinking of poverty, crime, ethnicity, race and the welfare state's available jobs at the lowest level for those "with connections," but I got the feeling this was not a popular topic to introduce. They would likely never get off the hill[23] anyway, although my oral history classes were intended to do just that."

Professor Buhle said he only had the one session at the ACI, but it was memorable. Buhle was quoted as saying "this is always the best audience."

To which a RI Reading official said, "It's a captive audience."

The inmates laughed.

Jerry had high praise for the program. "We're humans, too. We're not an illiterate bunch of fools here."

It would be several years before another path caught Jerry's intellectual, and spiritual, curiosity. This one would stay with him long after the last time he would be locked in a cell.

---

[23] College Hill where Brown University looks down in the city

Chapter 17 *Wicca and a New Path*

"People only see what they are prepared to see."
— *Ralph Waldo Emerson*

March 28, 1996, is a date Jerry will not soon forget. As he sat in New Hampshire State Prison for Men in Concord, New Hampshire, he was about to become associated with Witchcraft and Wicca.

It would change his life.

"There was a group there who were always talking about it. One Sunday morning, a friend of mine who was in that group asked me if I wanted to join. I said I wanted to observe. I didn't know anything about it, so I wasn't ready to jump in full force."

Those first moments experiencing the elements of Wicca made a significant impression on Jerry.

The administration of New Hampshire State Prison allowed outside guidance. Practitioners and experienced Wicca adherents guided the group and aided Jerry path of study.

Jerry found it fascinating.

"I said I wanted to come into the group. I became very interested and never looked back. In the history of my family, there are stories about vampires. Going back there were folks involved in Paganism, so it just felt so comfortable to me. I was raised Roman

Catholic and served as an altar boy, but never felt as comfortable as I have with Paganism."

For the first time Jerry thought about the things he'd done, the choices he'd made, and the opportunities he missed. By looking inside, he put the 'life' in perspective.

He'd been in prison for eighteen years. Eighteen years of the prime time in a man's life. His children had grown up without his physical presence, although he did more to stay involved with his kids than some men do who are outside prison walls. He had put aside most of his initial anger over his brother's conviction, given the realities he faced.

The first few moments listening to the group leader speak of the practices and doctrines of Wicca, Jerry knew he had found something positive on which to focus his efforts. It would lead him to understand there is a difference between speaking the truth and insisting people listen to it.

No one has the power to convince anyone of anything they are not ready to accept. The only thing you can do is accept the consequences of your choices and always seek to speak the truth to yourself. The immersion into the tenets and practices of Wicca opened Jerry's eyes to a whole new world and a new path in life.

It led him to tell his story as best he can, as honestly as he could, with no expectations.

Twenty years later he is still working at that craft, and still learning. He does not preach or force his thinking upon others but is happy to talk about it with anyone who would like to know more.

Wicca, also known as Pagan Witchcraft, blends ancient Paganism with twentieth-century Hermetic ideas. Gerald Gardner, a retired British civil servant, introduced it to the public in 1954. He developed the practice in writings and teachings during the 1940s and 50s.

Wicca is an open religion without a central authority.

It is described as an organization devoted to God and Goddess, focused on nature and the wonders of the elements. Members are Pagans who practice their faith with earth-centered values. Those who embrace Wicca are an eclectic group. They gather to strengthen their knowledge, to honor the cycles of the moon, and celebrate the eight holy days of the year.

The word 'witch' comes from the old English Wicce, meaning a female witch, and Wicca, a male witch.

During the rituals, Jerry feels pins and needles and goosebumps.

"That's telling me I'm feeling it. It began to make me calmer. It helped to alleviate stress. It puts me in a different place and a different frame of mind."

Jerry began his own group calling it The Coven of The Chalice and The Blade. His cousin, Diane, is more experienced than Jerry, so they make a good match. Jerry is the High Priest of the group.

"We don't care what your nationality is," he explains. "We don't seek out people like Catholics do. If someone is interested, they come to us. We don't force our will on anyone."

Jerry calls his people the new generation.

"We don't have a clue of what our ancestors did or how they did it. Personally, I don't care because there's nothing we can do about it."

They meet weekly for discussion and teachings. Learning Wicca is a process.

Less formal than Catholicism or other "traditional" religions, it is closer to learning to play a musical instrument. Initially, one is awkward and struggling. It takes time to overcome misconceptions and grasp the teachings. With practice, one develops as an adept of

Wicca. But, like a musical instrument, there is never an end to learning. It is a continuing process with revelations, intuitive understandings, setbacks, and mastering knowledge.

Wicca bears remarkable similarities to the meditation of Buddhists and other contemplative practices. One aspect of Wicca is the elements. Earth, Air, Fire, Water, and Spirit. Often represented by the pentagram or pyramid, the link to other related matters such as to know, to will, to dare, silence (keeping the practice within the circle because of past treatment of Wicca adherents and witches), and spirit (or ether.)

In the weekly session, Jerry acts as a teacher or guide, prompting the others with questions to probe their depth of understanding. In discussing the five elements, Jerry asks the question, "And what is the element I added to this?"

After a few moments, one of them comes up with the answer. Sunshine Tillinghast, Jerry's niece. She is the daughter of Jerry's older brother, John. Jerry's daughters, Vanessa and Kristian, also embrace the practice.

"To believe," says Sunshine.

Jerry nods. "Exactly, if you don't believe in this stuff, don't bother studying or reading it. Get up and walk away. If you don't believe, don't bother."

Does he recommend the Pagan philosophy to others?

"Absolutely. It's not for everyone but, until I sat in on that session all those years ago, I didn't know it was for me either. It's taught me to learn from the past, not live in it. And to embrace the future by focusing on the things I can do to make me, my life, and the lives of those around me better."

Chapter 18   *Five More Years*

Courtesy of the State Police Intelligence Unit

In 1994, the State Police Intelligence Unit was in a state of transition. Once focused almost exclusively on traditional organized crime, they now faced emerging criminal groups of a wider variety with differing backgrounds.

Yet their favorite target, organized crime, diminished but still very much alive, remained on their radar.

Former Rhode Island State Police Colonel Steven O'Donnell knew about Jerry and his brother Harold. At the time assigned to the State Police Intelligence Unit, O'Donnell and the other detectives spent a great deal of time focused on the mob. Before O'Donnell joined the State Police, he worked as a guard in the ACI.

He remembered Jerry as a disruptive force in prison and knew of his reputation as an enforcer for the Patriarca Crime family.

O'Donnell grew up in South Providence and began a life in law enforcement in 1983 when he was hired as a guard at the ACI, keeping watch over mobsters in the facility's maximum-security section. He became familiar with Jerry's older brother Harold, although neither had much interaction until O'Donnell joined the state police and Harold was on parole.

The intelligence unit created a false identity for O'Donnell, using the name Steve Foley, equipped him with phony IDs, and set him out to locations where he was likely to encounter mob-connected guys.

One of the best hunting grounds for mob guys and their associates is a courthouse.

Harold Tillinghast was out on parole for the Basmajian homicide having served fifteen years of his life sentence. The Parole Board was generally reluctant to release someone on such a serious charge.

Paul Dimaio attended every parole hearing for Harold. He attributes the early parole decision as indicative of the board's concerns about the original case against Harold.

The standard questions before the parole board are the likelihood of re-offending and whether the prisoner has been rehabilitated.

Dimaio raised the same point at each hearing. "He doesn't need rehabilitation, he's innocent."

Finally, based on a combination of factors including Harold's deteriorating health, he was granted parole. O'Donnell spotted Harold Tillinghast outside a courthouse in Providence.

Why Harold was at the court that day is lost to history, but O'Donnell, posing as Steve Foley, struck up a conversation with him. O'Donnell said they had been in prison at the same time and, although Harold didn't remember O'Donnell, he went along with the conversation.

O'Donnell told Harold he was a bookie and needed protection.

Harold put him in touch with Joseph Lema of East Providence, a criminal who would try to protect Foley for a fee. But the intelligence unit was after more significant players than Lema.

Each of these meetings took place with video and/or audio surveillance by other members of the Intelligence Unit.

Brendan Doherty, who rose to become Superintendent of the State Police several years before O'Donnell, was a sergeant in the intelligence unit. Lieutenant John Scungio was the officer in charge.

Because of the nature of this and other in-depth undercover investigations involving troopers, Doherty rewrote the department policy on covert operations requiring audio or video surveillance, or both whenever possible, for all undercover meetings.

After every meeting with a target, investigators would gather to evaluate the information and determine the next course of action.

In Harold's case, he was viewed as a doorway into the bigger organization. The Intelligence unit needed a plan to force Harold to introduce O'Donnell to other, more connected, players.

Investigators created a story to get Harold to contact his brother Jerry. Jerry, still in prison for the Basmajian murder and serving his time in New Hampshire, was pulled into the ploy. Jerry gave the order to leave Foley alone. The call Harold made to Jerry was recorded. So was a call O'Donnell made to Lema who told him not to worry, he would talk to Jerry about it.

As part of the State Police investigation, many calls were recorded. Based on those calls and other information the Intelligence Unit gathered, dozens of criminals were taken off the street.

NBC News in New York, researching a story on crime in New England, contacted Paul DiMaio, Jerry's long-time lawyer and asked for an interview with Jerry, who obliged. Here is part of that interview, conducted in DiMaio's Providence law office.

Jerry told the NBC reporter:

"Law enforcement, their job, no matter what level, is to take criminals off the street. A criminal, no matter what level, their job is not to let that happen. I hate praising police because I'm on the other side, but the State Police did a good job. They did it the right way.

"First off, O'Donnell was a corrections officer. The trooper knew the prison system and knew everything Harold was doing. So, when he turned around and said you were here, or you were there, he caught my brother sleeping. I hate to say it. Harold was caught off guard because he was trying to make money."

"When the police came to New Hampshire to bring Jerry back to court in Rhode Island, he was dumbfounded.

"I thought I was coming back for a parole hearing," Jerry said. "They take me to court and stick me in a cell with Harold and Lema. Once I figured out what was happening, I was pissed. I looked at the two of them and said, 'me one good reason I shouldn't turn this bullshit charge into a double homicide.'

"The two of them just stayed away. I was hot. My brother wasn't himself then, they took advantage of that."

It would cost Jerry early parole and add five more years to his sentence. Harold returned to prison on the parole violation and served several more years.

He died in 2004.

"All just part of the game," Jerry says. "All just part of the game. I pled guilty because I didn't know what else the State Police had or who they had it on. I just wanted to be done with it."

As for Harold's part in the case, Jerry had this to say.

"For my brother, it was a death sentence. The conditions in prison made him sicker."

231

Chapter 19 *What Drives Criminal Behavior?*

"The heart has its reasons which reason does not understand"

Blaise Pascal, Pensees

In the book, *Bad Men Do What Good Men Dream by Robert I. Simon, MD*[24] the author describes the prevalence of anti-social behavior and how it shows itself in the human population.

Three percent of males and one percent of females exhibit anti-social behavior. Typically, the behavior begins at age seven with boys and thirteen with girls.

In the general prison population of the United States, 50-80% of prisoners meet the criteria for anti-social personality disorder, and 15-30% meet the criteria for psychopathy[25].

---

[24] Bad Men Do What Good Men Dream. A Forensic Psychiatrist Illuminates the Darker Side of Human Behavior. By Robert I. Simon, MD. American Psychiatric Press, Inc. 1996 ISBN 0-88048-688-0
[25] Psychopathy is defined as mental illness or disorder

Anti-social boys most likely come from large families where they interact with other boys. In families with more girls than boys, something inhibits anti-social behavior.

Other factors are maternal deprivation in the first five years of life, insufficient nurturing, and lack of socialization skills. Often the father exhibits anti-social behavior and alcoholic tendencies.

Most psychiatrists agree that a combination of genetic, developmental, and environmental factors breed anti-social behavior.

How does this apply in Jerry's case? It's difficult to say. There are cases where all three factors are present, and children never exhibit anti-social behavior. There are other examples where none or just one or two were present and anti-social behavior occurred.

To understand how Jerry went from his youth in South Providence to a life sentence for a conviction of murder, one must look at several factors.

Jerry's enlistment in the Marine Corps opened a path away from the influences of the neighborhood and poverty. By all indications, had Jerry not become entangled in the incident in the hamlet of Song Tra II, and survived the rest of his tour in Viet Nam, he'd have remained in the Marine Corps.

In his written statement to the court-martial panel, Jerry asked for nothing more than a return to duty. He acknowledged his mistakes in not doing more to stop the rape. He accepted the demotion and loss of pay, but he wanted more than anything else to stay in the Marine Corps.

Experienced military officers, who later reviewed his file, argued charging him as an accessory to the crime was wrong.

Despite their recommendation to set aside the verdict, Jerry was sent to prison.

Sometimes, just one trigger brings anti-social behavior to the surface. Until that imposition of sentence in the court room in Viet Nam, Jerry's behavior matched his environment and friends. Nothing more than youthful juvenile indiscretions.

Once he ended up in the military prison, despite the efforts of many to right the wrong, it set his path. Ill-equipped to understand the geopolitics of Vietnam, and returning to the dangerous, corrupting environment he'd escaped with his enlistment, the lure of wise guys proved too much.

The lesson here is that while some men are born evil, more often outside factors and circumstances beyond their control set them on a path of criminal behavior.

Failing to understand this, compounded by glamorizing the "wise guy" lifestyle, is a self-fulfilling prophecy. By dealing with criminal behavior exclusively with jail sentences, absent meaningful rehabilitation, we delay, rather than prevent, continuing criminal conduct.

Putting men in prison, without offering a path to change, is a graduate program in criminality. It serves to bind them together in a common cause against society. We end up with men like Raymond Patriarca, Gerard Ouimette, and Jerry Tillinghast because, in a way, we made them.

Listen to the stories of these men and their experiences in prison. The common themes resonate. Taken under the wing of older inmates, making connections for when they get out, educating them in the ways of the street. They characterize almost every career criminal.

Jerry, in telling his story, recognizes he bears responsibility for his choices. Yet we must recognize our approach to criminal justice may limit the options people such as Jerry have when released.

Chapter 20   *Parole*

Gerald Martin Tillinghast walked out of prison in January 2007.

For close to thirty of his sixty-one years, Jerry was a prisoner where every day was controlled by someone else. Now, a free man for the first time since his arrest in 1978, Jerry had his life back.

But it was a different world.

All his children were now adults, some with families of their own.

His brother, Harold, was dead. He was fast approaching social security age. Yet, he was out of prison.

It was a brief taste of freedom.

He went to live with his sister Helen and her husband, Phil. Limited in his options, old habits emerged, and old associates offered an opportunity to make some money. They were not good options. He was part of what Rhode Island State Police called a "major bust" against the Patriarca Crime family.

In November 2008, while he was working at a Providence area flea market, Jerry and seventeen others were rounded up in a drug, gambling, and gun running ring at the Valley Flea Market and at a second-hand furniture store, Dyer Discount.

The headlines were a bit exaggerated, but it was a criminal case and not one a man on parole should be involved in.

One of those arrested was mobster Nicholas Pari, convicted of murdering Joe 'Onions' Scanlon in 1978. The case was the first in Rhode Island to result in a murder conviction without recovering the victim's body.

For years, rumors swirled about where Joey Onion's body was dumped. Tips came into various police agencies; Joey was in the trunk of a junked Caddy, they dumped Joey in the bay wrapped in a tarp, Joey's not dead, he's living in Vegas.

All of them proved fruitless. It was a conscience reawakened by the specter of death that finally unveiled the truth.

On his deathbed, Pari told police where he buried Scanlon; in a lot off Bullocks Point Avenue in East Providence. Surrounded by media, police finally found what was left of Joey Onions. Thirty plus years after his disappearance.

Jerry went back to prison for three and a half years awaiting trial. In 2011, he was released for time served after pleading guilty to a charge of selling knock-off brand sneakers. Not exactly a significant mob offense, but enough to complicate Jerry's already complicated life.

He could have gone back for the rest of his life, had he been convicted of the drug, gun and gambling charges.

Out for what he hoped will be for good, but on lifetime parole, Jerry was home again, living with his sister and her family in Cranston, Rhode Island.

Jerry turned 72 years of age on March 11, 2018.

Chapter 21 *Redemption*

Webster defines redemption as, "the act or process of serving to offset or compensate for a defect. Or a thing that saves someone from error or evil."

In simpler terms, to rehabilitate oneself before your fellow humans.

With Jerry Tillinghast, redemption may be elusive or impossible to those who know him only through headlines and news stories.

It may be unnecessary to family and friends who look past such notoriety.

But to Jerry, his act of redemption has taken place over the thirty years he spent in prison and the opportunity it afforded for close introspection.

Wicca and the tenets of that faith gave him something to embrace. Something to focus his innate intelligence stripped of the anger and resentment of all those past years.

Jerry made choices.

Some were made out of loyalty to family, like his brother Harold.

Some were made out of loyalty to Raymond L.S. Patriarca, who served as a surrogate father when his own father withheld parental affection.

Some were made out of greed, rage, or anger fueled by hanging around with the wiseguy crowd.

Some were made because he just didn't care.

None can be undone

The Jerry Tillinghast of today is a changed man. If others see him as no different from the Jerry Tillinghast of the past that it is outside his control.

All he can do is move forward. Recognize the errors of the past and apply the lessons to whatever life he has left.

In the Crimetown podcast on Providence, Jerry said, "My favorite word is choices. You make choices, and you live with the consequences."

His choices had consequences. For Jerry, they cost him thirty years in prison away from his family. For his brother, Harold, Jerry's choices may well have cost him his life.

It is easy to say one will accept the consequences of your choices before you make them. It is a whole other thing to look back through the lens of hindsight.

The choices seemed natural at the moment. The consequences were not. Time has come for Jerry to explain the real cost of those choices.

Chapter 22 *Rest of the Story*

Basmajian Timeline

To understand the complexities and contradictions in the case, a timeline of that evening will put the events in perspective.

Timeline of Basmajian Homicide November 30, 1978

(Times are from trial transcripts, police reports, and reconstruction based on the testimony of investigators.)

3:50-5:15 p.m.

Surveillance initiated (6 members from RI State Police and FBI later reduced to three; two from State Police, one from FBI.)

Basmajian and his wife go to RI Registry in Providence. Wife driving Lincoln with RI Dealer plate 109D. Leave registry and drive to wife's father's house stopping at a Chinese restaurant in Johnston.

5:15 p.m.

Basmajian leaves house and drives to the same Chinese restaurant in Johnston. Meets with David Cianci.

5:45-6:00 p.m.

Basmajian and Cianci drive to Michael's Lounge. JT-249 (Jerry Tillinghast's car) parked in front of Michael's.

5:45-6:15 p.m.

Basmajian and Cianci leave Michael's and drive to Lisa's Restaurant Johnston.

6:48-7:00 p.m.

Basmajian leaves Lisa's alone and returns to Michael's Lounge.

7:00-7:15 p.m.

Jerry Tillinghast and Basmajian walk out of Michael's Lounge and talk on the sidewalk. Tillinghast and Basmajian go back inside Michael's. Basmajian emerges a moment later, enters his vehicle, and drives away.

7:20-7:25 p.m.

Jerry Tillinghast back outside Michael's pacing up and down the sidewalk. Walks to a pay phone and makes a call. Returns to Michael's

8:00-8:05 p.m.

RI Reg AX-134 drives by Michael's (Harold Tillinghast's car) Jerry Tillinghast back outside Michael's waves at someone in IRS parking lot across the street from Michael's. Harold meets with Jerry, and both go inside Michael's.

Basmajian returns, parks his car on Barclay street. He had changed clothing. Jerry Tillinghast comes out of Michael's and meets with Basmajian. They both look in the trunk of Basmajian's car. Investigators cannot see into the trunk from their position.

8:05-9:15 p.m.

Basmajian and Jerry Tillinghast leave Michael's in Basmajian's car. Investigators testify they do not see Harold Tillinghast at that time.

One surveillance car drove around the block ending up in front of Basmajian on Broadway. Basmajian turns off Broadway onto DePasquale Avenue. Investigators try to locate the vehicle again but cannot find it.

Surveillance cars head to Johnston in an attempt to locate the vehicle. Not found in Johnston.

Surveillance cars then head to St. Rocco's Club on Fourth Avenue, Cranston.

Lt. Vespia of the State Police parks in the lot of the bowling alley on Elmwood Avenue, half a mile from St. Rocco's

Yellow 1974 Mercury sedan drives past Lt. Vespia from the rear of the bowling alley. Dealer plate attached to vehicle partially visible are two number, 1 and 0, rest not visible. Three men in the car. Jerry Tillinghast is driving, Harold Tillinghast in passenger front seat, Basmajian in the back seat.

Mercury turns onto Elmwood Ave, then Rte. 10 South, to 95 South. Takes Exit 13, Airport Connector. Three silhouettes in the Mercury. Investigators' view is momentarily blocked by a snow fence along the exit ramp.

9:15 p.m.

Mercury is stopped at red light Post Road and Airport Connector. Two silhouettes visible in the car, both in the front seat.

Mercury turns left on Post Road then right onto Fullerton Street. Surveillance cars did not follow.

9:20 p.m.

Surveillance cars drive into the area of Fullerton Street, Mercury is located behind National Car Rental building on Fresno Road. Basmajian is dead/dying lying on the driver's side back seat of the vehicle. No one else is in the area.

One surveillance car stays with the body. Lt. Vespia and Special Agent Reilly of the FBI went to St. Rocco's to locate the Tillinghasts. They were not there.

9:50-9:55 p.m.

Vespia and Reilly then went to Michael's Lounge and arrested Jerry and Harold.

Silent No More...

Since November 30, 1978, until this very moment, Jerry has made one invariable statement on the Basmajian homicide.

Harold was not there. Harold was not in the car.

In Jerry's words, for the first time, he reveals the rest of the story.

"A couple days before Bas was killed, I always called him Bas, I met with Gerard (Ouimette), Johnny (Ouimette), and Skippy (Byrnes) at St. Rocco's. We always met at St. Rocco's to plan things. After small talk at the bar, the four of us gathered around the pool table. People knew enough to stay away when Gerard held a meeting. No one could hear what we said. If they were smart, no one wanted to listen to what we said.

"Gerard told us there was a couple of freelance bookies we were gonna rob. He told Skippy and me to get Bas and take care of it. Skippy said he'd get a car, meaning steal one, and park it at the bowling alley on Elmwood Ave. We picked the following Thursday to do the job.

"I got a hold of Bas. We planned to meet at Michael's, then drive to meet Skippy. When Thursday came, Bas showed up early, and I wasn't around. He told Harold he'd be back. After I got there, I kept going outside to wait for him. Now he was late as usual. I walked to the phone booth down the street from Michael's and called Gerard. I told him 'Bas ain't here, we'll do this another night.'

"Just then Bas drove up, parked his car on the side street, and went inside Michael's. I went inside and met him. We left in his car a couple of minutes later and drove to the bowling alley to meet Skippy.

"Here's the thing, we discussed the plan to stash the car behind the bowling alley around the pool table in St. Rocco's and

244

no place else. We found out later, through a private detective named Richard Lane, who was working on the Joe Timpani case, that the police or FBI had a bug in the light over the table.

"There's no fucking way in hell they just happened to go to the bowling alley. Listen, Vespia and those guys were smart cops, they were good at what they did, but there's no way they just picked there to wait for us. They knew, somebody knew, or somebody told them we had the car there and that's why they went there looking for us.

"Look, just think about the shit the FBI pulled in Boston with Whitey. They were capable of anything back then to take us down. It's all part of the game, I accepted that. But where does it stop? My brother got screwed for something he never did.

"I know Gerard never talked. Skippy never talked. Johnny never talked. No one else heard us talk about it. It was the only way or the biggest fucking coincidence in the world.

"Anyway, we left Michael's. I told Bas to turn down a one-way street. He looked at me like I was nuts, but I told him just do it, if anyone's following us they'll have to commit, and we'll know. That's when they must have lost us. I never saw them, so I'll give 'em this, they were good at following us.

"Then again, they knew where we were going.

"We went to St. Rocco's, picked up Skippy, and went to the bowling alley. Skippy pointed out the car, so Bas parked, and we jumped in the stolen car. Skippy asked me to drive, he got in the passenger side, and Bas got in back. While we were sitting in the car, Skippy pulled out a gun and handed it to Bas.

"At the time I didn't think anything of it. I knew the three of us could handle pretty much anybody. Bas was a black belt and a real tough guy, but a little extra protection wasn't a bad idea. Later, when I had time to think about it, I knew why Skippy did it.

"Anyway, we pulled out of the lot and headed to 95. Skippy was the one who supposedly knew where we were going so he gave me directions. As we took the Airport Connector, I saw Skippy slide his gun out, cock it, and hold it toward the floor. I continued driving toward Post Rd.

"Just before we got to the red light, Skippy spun around and put three quick rounds into Bas's chest.

"I yelled, 'what the fuck, Skippy, what the fuck.'

'Orders, Jerry, orders' he said.

"I couldn't see Bas anymore, he was down on the seat behind me. Skippy told me where to turn, and we pulled behind the National Car Rental building. I jumped out of the car, not sure what was next. I didn't have a gun, but if Skippy went for me he'd have a big fight on his hands.

"Skippy opened the back door and put six more rounds into Bas. He must have reloaded while I was trying to figure out what the fuck was happening. He grabbed the gun he gave Bas. There was nothing more for me to do. A car pulled up and took us to St. Rocco's. Gerard came out, hugged me, then told the guy to drop me off at Michael's.

"I walked into Michael's. My brother Harold was sitting at a table with Paul DiMaio. I sat down with them. Next thing I knew, Vinnie Vespia came in, threw me up against the wall and told me I was under arrest for killing Bas. I didn't argue or resist, and I didn't say anything.

"Harold kept asking him why they were arresting me. I said Harold, 'Listen to me, you remember what I look like leaving here. Stay with Paul.'

"Vespia took me outside. The FBI guy, Reilly, said, 'We got what we wanted.' Vespia said, 'No, we need one more.'

"Meanwhile, Paul Dimaio came out to talk to the police.

246

Harold stuck his head out the door, yelling at the cops. Reilly and Vespia arrested him, put him in the car, and drove us to Scituate.

"After we were fingerprinted and photographed, they put us in a holding cell. I couldn't tell my brother what had happened, so all I said was 'you're over twenty-one buddy, a big boy. Keep your mouth shut, and we'll figure this out.'

"All throughout the trial, I expected a split verdict. Guilty for me. Not Guilty for Harold. What happened to him is a travesty. They tried to use him to get me to flip. Not the way I am. Harold was a big boy. He knew I'd never talk, and he never expected me to. But he should have let Paul testify.

"The jury might have doubts about all the others who testified about him being there the whole time, but they'd never doubt Paul. He wouldn't lie. He was upfront with the police. He told them Harold never left and that he couldn't be sure about me. That was the truth.

"Neither the state nor the defense listed him as a potential witness. Why? Why not call one of the most credible witnesses to the whole thing?

"They screwed my brother trying to get to Gerard through me. I don't care what anybody else did. What anybody else said to save their own ass. I keep my secrets because my word is my bond.

"After I was convicted, I had lots of time to think. Why whack Bas? Why that way?

"I finally made sense of it once I got over the anger of the trial.

"A few months before the shooting, Bas had made a big score. He was also running some deals with New York that Gerard didn't approve. Gerard borrowed twenty-five or thirty thousand from Bas.

"Bas asked me to help him get it back.

'Not my problem,' I said. 'I told you not to give him the money.'

"Gerard could be like that sometimes. He was greedy. Others noticed the things Bas was doing and didn't like it either. Gerard got the word to solve the problem. In a way, Bas paid for his own hit.

"They needed a way to get rid of him, but they also knew he was a dangerous guy.

"He wouldn't go easy.

"The whole story about robbing the bookies was just to get me and Bas to go along with them. They knew he might not trust Gerard and Skippy, but he'd believe me. They used me to get to Bas. If I'd have known they were gonna kill him, I would've walked away. I would have warned Bas. He was my friend. They used that friendship to lure him in.

"Byrnes gave Bas the gun to make him relax, take him off his guard. Why would a guy who planned to kill you give you a gun? I heard later the bullets in the weapon Skippy gave Bas had been crimped so they wouldn't fire.

"Bas never saw it coming. He probably figured he'd get the money Gerard owed him from the score that night.

"It was a treacherous world I lived in back then. I see that now. There were some real bad guys involved. But it doesn't justify convicting someone of a crime they didn't commit.

"I know they thought of it as a crusade but, if they're supposed to be the good guys, where's the line drawn on what they can do?

"Look, their job was to arrest us. Our job was to not let that happen. We all played by different rules back then but there must be a line that is not crossed. Putting Harold in prison killed him. Not right away, but the environment in the joint wrecked his health. It was a death sentence for an innocent man.

"I don't care who gets pissed off. I don't care what anybody else thinks about me. I do care that the cops and prosecutors were willing to let an innocent man die in jail for their so-called crusade."

More Questions Than Answers

Taken alone, each of the inconsistencies in the reports, bail hearing record, trial testimony, and news reports can be explained or ignored.

But taken together, it gives one pause.

Add in the litany of things the FBI did during that era to target organized crime in New England and one must wonder. Was the real story the one that unfolded in the court room almost forty years ago or is it the story revealed in this book?

Was this a case of the ends justifying the means? Taking two bad guys off the street, whether they were both guilty or not?

Or was it a case of mistaken identity based on likely, but incorrect, assumptions that it must have been Harold Tillinghast in that shadowy passenger side seat?

With Harold long dead and the case fading into the past, the full truth may never be known.

But consider this, why choose now to tell his side of the story? There is little for him to gain here. One must look at the big picture to understand his choice to speak after all these years. He is facing the realities of mortality. He is coming to terms with all those choices he wished he could undo.

Jerry is the one remaining person left who was in the car that night. He's had time to consider all those moments that led him to this point in life.

He could go silently into that good night. Or, he could rage against the injustice.

The one thing he has left is to be silent no more.

Why should we listen to him? Why should we take the word of a convicted murderer, a felon, a feared mob enforcer?

Because we can learn something from it.

There is truth embedded with consistency. Jerry's claim that Harold was not in the car has never wavered. Even Incremental revelations add up over time.

Jerry freely admits to driving the stolen car, his part in the aftermath of the shooting, and to keeping the truth to himself for all these years because of his personal beliefs.

We owe it to ourselves and the pursuit of Justice to at least listen.

Afterthoughts

All humans change. We are never the same person throughout our lives. We all have a dual persona; one public and one private. For those, through circumstances or intention, thrust into the broader public stage, these two evolving versions are more distinct.

And so it is with Gerald Martin 'Jerry' Tillinghast.

There is the reputed and feared mob enforcer, the convicted murderer, the member of the Gerard Ouimette crew of the Patriarca Crime family. The notoriety of infamy has persistent longevity. As Shakespeare said, "The evil that men do lives after them; the good is oft interred with their bones."

There is the private Gerald Martin Tillinghast of today; Marine, Vietnam veteran, sponsor, organizer, and manager of an annual fundraiser for veterans. He is a father, a grandfather, and a friend to a broad spectrum of people.

I, like many others in Rhode Island, knew about the notorious version. Jerry Tillinghast the mob guy. The Bonded Vault robber who convinced a jury to find him not guilty. The prison rabble-rouser moved from state to state to minimize his influence in prison.

Jerry Tillinghast the convicted murderer.

Prisons, absent meaningful rehabilitation, are finishing schools for criminality. They are a self-fulfilling prophecy where we send our most disadvantaged and then turn a blind eye while they are systematically selected by more experienced criminals.

Organized crime, be it the once powerful Mafia or the newest iteration of hierarchical crime groups, need the fearlessness and recklessness of the unguided. We are sowing the seeds for criminal organizations to harvest a never-ending crop of eager and immature talent ripe for the picking.

Jerry and others like him are the proof.

251

While writing this book, I've come to know the other Jerry Tillinghast. There is no doubt in my mind a civil conversation with the more infamous public version would be of a different tone, if not impossible. I can, however, say without hesitation I've gained something from my conversations with today's Jerry Tillinghast.

Life often sends people down paths **not** of their own choosing. Some are as much a victim as other, more sympathetic, souls.

His experiences in Vietnam started Jerry down a rabbit hole of bad decisions. We taught him to kill, numbed him to empathy for human life, and then sacrificed him on the altar of a failed policy in Vietnam. We may not prevent it from happening in every case, but we should recognize veterans need as much support returning from the battle as we offer them in battle.

This is not to excuse the things Jerry did or may have done. It is a telling of the whole story. It may enlighten us enough to open our eyes to do as much as we can to change things going forward.

Jerry would be the first to tell you he doesn't want sympathy. He made choices, and he lives every day with the consequences. But he will tell you that from the moment his world collapsed in Vietnam, it set in motion many things beyond his control.

A balanced analysis of the totality of circumstances and evidence supports that.

If we don't want to create more men like Jerry Tillinghast, we must learn from his experiences.

To twist Shakespeare words,

Some are born evil, some achieve evil, and some have evil thrust upon them.

About the Author

Joe Broadmeadow retired with the rank of captain from the East Providence, Rhode Island Police Department after twenty years. He served in the various divisions within the department, including Commander of Investigative Services. He also worked in the Organized Crime Drug Enforcement Task Force (OCDETF) and on special assignment to the FBI Drug Task Force.

Choices: You Make 'em You Own 'em is Joe's first non-fiction work. He is the author of three works of fiction. *Silenced Justice* and *Collision Course,* featuring East Providence Police Detective Lieutenant Josh Williams, and *A Change of Hate*, a spin-off of the Josh Williams series, featuring Defense Attorney Harrison 'Hawk' Bennett.

The books continue to garner rave reviews and are available on Amazon.com

When Joe is not writing, he is hiking or fishing (and thinking about writing). Joe completed a 2,185-mile thru-hike of the Appalachian Trail in September 2014. After completing the trail, Joe published a short story, *Spirit of the Trail,* available on Amazon.
Thanks for reading! Please take a moment to review the book, it is most appreciated.
http://www.amazon.com/Joe-Broadmeadow/e/B00OWPE9GU

Contact the author: joe.broadmeadow@hotmail.com
Website: www.authorjoebroadmeadow.com
Twitter: @JBroadmeadow
Author Blogs: www.joebroadmeadowblog.wordpress.com

Special Thanks to friends and supporters

I want to take this opportunity to thank my friends and family for their support. I would also like to mention a few places who have graced me with their hospitality and welcomed me to their fine establishments.

Harriet's Kitchen, Cranston, RI

Marchetti's, Cranston, RI

Runway 41, Warwick, RI

Amedeo's, Cranston, RI

Ciara's, Johnston, RI

Avenue Grille, North Providence, RI

Thanks to all of you for everything.

Jerry Tillinghast
Facebook link: https://www.facebook.com/jerry.tillinghast.5